Widowoman – A Journey

An insider's experience of the cultural phenomenon "widow" and dealing with loss in our society and the Signposts along the way.

By

Sharon Womack Doty

Arpeggias, LLC

3002 N. Cleveland, #12

Enid, OK 73703

swdarpeggias@gmail.com

ISBNs 978-0-9770953-7-7

ACKNOWLEDGEMENT

After reading the book you will know that there are many people for me to acknowledge on this journey. My children and grandchildren are the reason this book exists. They would not let me go on with life without sharing this experience with others. The support and love from my friend Leslie Zieren cannot be adequately appreciated in these pages. In addition to these amazing people and the others who so richly impacted my life since Ned's death, there is a group of people who always listen to me as bigger than I know myself to be and hold me accountable for their listening of me. To Suzy, Ann, Jeffrey, Scott, Jaime, Avanish, Mickye, Mario, Casey, David, Stephen, AB, Nancy, and Kathy B, thank you for counting on me to show up in life as the possibility of possibility and for never settling for anything less. Your stand for me and the difference I am committed to making with this book is a daily, unwavering reminder that giving my word and honoring that word has life work.

THE JOURNEY BEGINS

At 3:22 a.m. on March 23, 2011, I was a "Sadie."

Now, for those who are not musical comedy buffs, according to Fannie Brice in *Funny Girl*, a "Sadie" is a married lady and for years I had referred to being married that way because Fanny was a strong woman who also had a great love and not many illusions about what it looked like to truly make it work. So, until that moment, I was a "Sadie" and my husband, Ned, and I were just a few short weeks away from celebrating 45 years of living and loving each other.

At 3:23 a.m., I was suddenly something the culture refers to as a "widow."

The death certificate says he "officially" died several minutes later, but in that moment when he sat on the side of the bed and suddenly fell over on me, waking me up from a sound sleep, he was gone at 3:23 on 3/23.

I was now in uncharted territory, entering a new cultural paradigm, and virtually everything in my life would change. Nothing would ever be the same. I soon discovered that I had no idea what that would mean for life as I knew it before that day.

The next hour of my life is burned into my memory. I can recall with unimaginable clarity every moment that passed between the time I was awakened by his body collapsing on mine and the moment I kissed him goodbye for the final time in the hospital ER. Some of these memories make me smile and some spark a steady stream of tears in my eyes.

I called 911 and I remember working really hard to follow the instructions from the operator to get my naked, dead husband off the bed onto the floor. I remember being worried about ridiculous things as I was pulling and tugging on his limp body. First, there was the fact that he sleeps in the nude. What were the first responders going to think when they saw this 67-year-old man naked on the floor? Second, when he collapsed, he had been sitting up on the bedside to use his urinal and death did not take away that need, so there I was – pulling on Ned to get him to the floor and the pool of urine on the bed and floor was continuing to grow. I was worried about the hardwood floors getting ruined and him plopping in the puddle and getting urine all over himself and how could I clean him up because he would hate being seen like that.

Then, there was my concern that pulling on him was twisting his body and I might break his arm. I remember laughing as I struggled to move his 200-plus pounds of truly dead weight and at the same time I was waiting for him to wake up and laugh with me. After all, playing dead so that I had to work hard to get him moved was just the kind of thing he would do because he thought it was funny. But it wasn't a joke – it was not funny at all – the love of my life was gone and would not be coming home to me again.

The teams of first responders that came to my house were wonderful. The neighbors across the street saw the emergency vehicle lights and came over to help. My dear friend, Leslie, and my son, Ted, arrived within minutes to lead me through the next hour with gentleness, love, and grace – and just a touch or two of the humor that was so much part of the flavor of my Ned's life. When I called her, Leslie answered immediately, and lived only a block away. Not so with my son. He sleeps with a CPAP, so I had to call his wife Treasure's phone several times to wake them up to tell them what was happening, but once Ted was awake, he came over quickly.

My son gave me a bit of good-natured ribbing about making the EMTs cover Ned with a sheet. You see, my husband preferred not to wear clothes. In fact, as the kids reminded me at the funeral, one of his life theories was "clothes are optional" as long as we were home alone. Ted joked with me that Dad would have thought at least this one last time I would let him go out the front door in his birthday suit. I smiled and said, "Not happening on my watch and he knows it." Ted smiled back and hugged me as they wheeled his dad out the door of our home of 25 years for the last time.

I remember what I was wearing, and that shirt is still hanging in my closet. Every time I see it, I am reminded of that night. I will never forget my friend Captain Wes Duckett from the Tulsa Fire Department coming in to express his condolences when the crew left the hospital ER. Ned and I knew Wes, and I was grateful that it was his team that took care of my man that night. A couple of weeks later, I wrote to the Fire Chief and to the head of EMSA, the ambulance service, to ask them to pass on my appreciation to the teams that came that night. They were respectful, professional and kind beyond measure and I wanted them to know I noticed and was grateful for their work. A few months later, Wes contacted me to let me know he was now operating a lawn service on his days off and that he would like to include mowing my yard if I wanted. It was a remarkable offer because I lived on a third of an acre and he offered to mow it weekly for $40. He did that for the next three years that I lived in the house and never raised my rate.

Along with our son, Ted, Ned and I had two daughters, Shannon, who also lived in Tulsa, and Erica who lived near Kansas City, Missouri. Shannon met us at the hospital. Erica had much further to come. By the time she got to Tulsa from Kansas City, Ned was already gone from the room in the ER. She would not get the chance to see him one last time until the next day.

The hospital staff was gentle and caring. I was so grateful that we were the only ones there at that time. They let us stay in one of the empty spaces while they took care of Ned and officially pronounced him dead. While we were waiting, Shannon's husband, my son-in-law, Brian, found Father Steve, our parish priest and good friend of Ned's, who came to be with us and give Ned the one last blessing of his life on earth.

The hospital staff informed me that Ned was an organ donor, and I was glad that some of the body that had housed his life would go on to help someone else have a better life. The representative of the organization was very kind and compassionate on the phone that night as she explained to me what would be happening next with his body. Later they sent me a beautiful metal paperweight with a butterfly design, and I look at it every day. It always makes me smile as a reminder that some part of him is still making a difference somewhere in another's world. In life, after he had a stroke, it took 13 different medications every day to keep that body going. In death, the body that housed his life is giving life over and over to others in need. How beautiful is that?

The next part of the day is a big blur. I know I went home and started making calls and that family started arriving. The time between leaving the hospital and the final trip with the kids to the funeral home the next day was filled with people visiting and calling, food deliveries, attempts to nap, questions, phone calls to Ned's sisters, and the daunting first visit to the funeral home to make decisions I wish Ned had made earlier.

My brothers and my sisters-in-law were great. They hugged and held me close and watched carefully to make sure I was okay. One of them called my doctor and ordered one sleeping pill because he was concerned that I would not be able to sleep. He need not have worried. For the first time since Ned's stroke four years earlier, I knew I could go to sleep without being concerned that Ned was not going to make it through the night. That part of the journey of my life was over, and I could rest because I knew that finally he could.

I remember that the first thing I asked Ted to do when we got home from the hospital was to take the wheelchair and walker Ned had used to the garage. Ned did not need them anymore and I did not want to see them and continue to be reminded of what he had been dealing with since the stroke. He was free of them now and I wanted to be also. I don't think that everyone understood those actions right away but frankly it was not up to me to explain to them why I wanted that stuff out of my house. My love was no longer bound by the body he was stuck in for the four years before his death and I wanted the reminders of that struggle gone from the house.

That first day all we could do was plan and talk and deal with what was happening moment by moment. I was aware of lots of eyes on me all the time. People were worried about me, but I was fine – at least as fine as I could be in the situation. Looking back on that day I can see that I dealt with what was happening many different ways – and that is really okay.

In 1996 I participated in a personal development program called the Landmark Forum. Ned also participated and we worked together with others in Landmark for many years. In fact, I have led seminars for Landmark since 2000 and, during 2011, I was participating in a worldwide training. One of my responsibilities during the training was to record the training calls and send them out to everyone the next day. I remember that I came home from the hospital and sent an email to the Landmark Seminar leaders who were part of that program to let them know that I would not be sending out the recording I had made from the training session the night before right away. In response I was inundated with calls of support and love and compassion from an amazing group of people who live life from, and for, what's possible – and who were stunned that I came home from saying goodbye to my husband and sent them an email about a recording being late.

I can now see that this is what my mind needed to focus on in that moment to survive the pain of the loss. I needed to have something to do that was ordinary and fairly mundane. There was much ahead of me that was going to challenge every fiber of my being. I could do this and feel like something was getting accomplished – so I did.

There were a lot of people and phone traffic in my house within the hour of coming home. Family started to arrive – and I have a big family – and friends came to support me and find out what was needed.

About 11 a.m. the phone rang again, and it was a friend from the Landmark community, Jerry Burkhart. Jerry is a Landmark Forum Leader and had worked with me in the Seminar Leader program for several years. Like others who called that day and the days after, he wanted to support me in whatever I needed. His words that day made a profound difference in how I was able to deal with what was happening. Those words still resonate with me today. He said that he had only been married a few years but that he could not imagine anything better at the end of his life than dying in the arms of the woman he had loved for 45 years. Ned got to do just that. It was such a comforting and peaceful context through which to view everything that happened the night before. That comment has stayed with me through good times and bad over the years since Ned died. There is comfort in knowing that he died in the arms of the woman he had loved for 45 five years and who had loved him all that time also.

Signposts[1]:

For the Widow: Let people love and support you on that day – and do whatever you need to do to take care of yourself.

For the Widow and Others Experiencing Loss: An ordinary or mundane task can assist you in recovering your equilibrium in the midst of the chaos of loss.

---

[1] This book is about journey and at the end of each chapter I will include a short signpost for you to consider on your trip.

THE NEXT STEP – FUNERAL PREPARATION

Ned died on Wednesday and when I asked Fr. Steve and the funeral home if the services could be on Friday, some were surprised.

They were worried that there was not enough time for people to make arrangements to come. However, one of my brothers, Dick, knew and even told other members of the family before he even talked to me that he was sure that is what I would do if I could. He knew that for me the waiting to get through the service would be the longest and hardest part. He knew that laying Ned to rest was something I would want for Ned and for the rest of the family and the people close to us. The only consideration was making sure that Ned's sister, Stacey, could get to Tulsa from Florida on such short notice. When that was confirmed, we set the date and time for Friday at 2:00 p.m. and started the process of letting everyone know.

He was gone and he was not coming back. Waiting for the service to have everything final was hard. We needed closure and to begin to discover what living life without him would be.

Fr. Steve was great. He came over a couple of times to meet with everyone in the family who wanted to talk to him. We talked about scriptures, music, and what we wanted in the service. We also talked about what the Church wanted and how to make use of all the amazing musical talent in our family. We shared stories of Ned and our life together as a family. We shared about his trains and his talents as an architect and his overwhelming love for his grandchildren. You know, that was the best of his life – being Papa to those grandkids – eight of them. We laughed. We cried. We leaned on each other and we did what had to be done to create a celebration of his life that honored all that he was and gave comfort to the whole family.

Ned had been approaching his 25th anniversary as a Permanent Deacon so there was some consideration about clergy being at the service, but for me, the Doty/Womack Clan and our friends were first and foremost in our minds and consideration. There were some of those clergy that we really did not want to be there and some we absolutely wanted, and we wanted Fr. Steve at the altar.

Fr. Steve did everything he could to make sure that those priests who were a significant part of Ned's faith life and Deaconate ministry had the opportunity to share in that day and be part of this celebration of his life. It meant a great deal that Father Jerry and Father Martin were also celebrating with us that day. The only one missing was Fr. Matt and he was out of town. His communication to us was beautiful and loving and he let us know that he too would miss this remarkable man named Ned Doty.

Moore Funeral Home was wonderful. The staff was kind and gracious and very helpful and, in the process, I learned something very valuable. Make a plan for your family to follow. Don't leave them with these decisions while they are grieving the loss of you. Making a plan is a gift to them. It does not mean that you are planning to die. It just means that you are taking care of matters they should not be burdened with while they are also dealing with the loss of someone they loved deeply.

I was dealing with the loss of my husband, and my children were dealing with the loss of their father, and we had to decide things like whether to embalm him and how many police escorts and limousines we needed as well as what music to use, the scriptures we wanted read, and much, much more. If you want to be buried, don't leave it to your family to buy a burial plot at the "time of need." It's the most expensive time to do that and once again they are required to turn their attention to other than what they are most present to – the grief and loss of losing you. These things must be decided, and it can all be done in advance. If you love your family – plan ahead.

Ned refused to consider these matters and we were left making all the decisions when our minds and hearts were reeling with the shock of losing him. He also did not have an Advanced Health Care Directive. He was afraid that meant that he was giving up on life. During these days I discovered that taking care of these matters in advance is a responsible, caring, loving thing to do for your family.

Among the tasks that have to be done at the time of the death is choosing what your loved one should be buried in. Another question was unexpected, but both these things were easy for me to answer. The funeral home wanted to know whether I wanted to keep his wedding ring. Deciding what he should wear and what to do with his wedding ring were simple.

Ned was an Ordained Permanent Deacon in the Catholic Church and, as I said, he died just a few months short of the 25th anniversary of his ordination. Those ordination vestments and the wedding ring I put on his finger 45 years earlier were two things of Ned's that I never wanted anyone else to have. So, I was clear that he would be buried with both. His wedding ring would be with him always and so would his ordination vestments.

When the funeral home let us know that Ned's body was back from the lab, we set off to take the vestments to the funeral director and give the rest of the family an opportunity to see him and say one last goodbye. However, this simple trip served as a reminder to us that Ned's unique sense of humor was still part of our lives. That he was no longer here did not mean that the humor – or his particular brand of it - stopped – even at the funeral home.

Our daughter, Erica, my sons-in-law, Brian and Chris, and my daughter-in-law, Treasure, were not at the hospital with us on Wednesday morning when Shannon, Ted, Leslie, and I had a chance to say our goodbyes. Erica and her husband Chris were at their home in in Missouri and Brian and Treasure were in their homes with their children while we were at the hospital.

Erica, Brian, and Treasure wanted an opportunity to view the body one last time, so we all went together to the funeral home on Thursday afternoon. They went to see Ned. The rest of us went along to take things to the funeral director that he needed to prepare the body for burial and to provide moral support.

So, we piled in the cars and off we went – me, Ted, Erica, Treasure, Chris, Shannon, and Brian. When we arrived at the home the kids asked to see Ned and the lovely grey-haired lady who it seems has worked at the funeral home for decades took Erica, Treasure, and Brian upstairs to see "Dad".

It seemed like only a few minutes later when the rest of us heard people running down the stairs. We looked up to see the funeral home staff member rushing red-faced into the office and grabbing the phone. Erica, Brian, and Treasure were right behind her - laughing. Before we could ask what happened we heard the secretary say, in a very shaky voice, into the phone receiver, "Terry, where is Mr. Doty?"

Turns out, they lost track of Ned's body and … the body they took the kids to see was not Ned's!

Instead, it was an older silver-haired man who looked a bit like Ned, and the kids were a little unsure because they did not know if the bloated belly and the brown spots were a result of the harvesting of the organs and the fact that he had now been gone for over 30 hours. Then, Brian blurted out, "This is not Dad!" and Erica said, "I'm so glad you said that!" She knew it wasn't Ned, but she was confused because the funeral home said it was and he had been to the lab. She thought something might have happened to him there. He looked really different – and she could not see his face right when they walked into the room. It was the right hair color, right body type, right age – but everything else was wrong. This was her dad?

The mortified funeral home staff person then took the kids on a search through the rooms upstairs looking for Ned only to find that he was not there.

At that point, Shannon's husband, Brian, said to the funeral home staffer, "Did you check Home Depot? He was always going off there to wander around without telling anyone." My family burst into laughter. The staff person was horrified and embarrassed, but we were sure Ned was there with us and was in on the joke.

This was a completely reasonable assumption on Brian's part. One of the things everyone knew about Ned was that he was reliable for just wandering off to places that interested him. At the flea market, the antique mall, the grocery store, or the theatre, he would just get distracted by something and go off on his own without telling anyone he was leaving. His favorite place in Tulsa to wander through was the Home Depot downtown. When it first opened, he spent most of the next three days wandering the aisles of that store and if there was ever a time I could not find him, I would call him and ask if he was at Home Depot. The answer was usually "Yes." The family learned early on that he would find his way back and there was no point in bringing it up because it was not going to change anything.

A few minutes later the funeral home located his body – in a freight elevator! It seems he was still making his way back from the lab – no surprise. So, the kids had their last "moment" with Ned in a freight elevator at the funeral home. This is more fitting that you can even imagine, and I know Ned would have loved it!

Erica's curiosity did provide us with the answer to a question we did not know we had. We found why caskets are often only open from the waist up – particularly if the person is a donor.

Erica has always had a somewhat morbid curiosity about things most of us don't have any interest in. She wants to see the disgusting spider bite that is rotting away your leg. Before I had knee replacement surgery, she watched one on video. She wanted to examine the gallstones that were found in my gall bladder.

On this occasion she wanted to see why the sheet was flat at the end of Ned's body where his feet would normally hold it up, so she started to raise the sheet to look at his feet. Treasure told her to stop – that they were told not to touch the body – but that did not stop Erica. After all, it was her dad and he was dead, and she wanted to know where his feet went.

As the kids came out of the freight elevator, Treasure told Ted that Erica lifted the sheet over Ned to look at his feet because it looked like he did not have any. We found out that the lab took skin and muscle to be used in operations on others in need, such as burn victims, so there were no tendons left in his legs to hold his feet up. Hmmm!

Erica's curiosity also provided us with the answer to a question we did not know we had about what the harvested skin, tendons, and muscles would be used for. Even all these years later I am reminded often of the wonderful gift it is to others when someone is a donor.

Signposts:

For the Widow and Others Experiencing Loss:

Create a plan for your family. Write it down and let them know it is done.

Don't suppress your sense of humor because of what others might think. The sadness and grief will be there for a long time. Be glad to share the moments and memories of joy and laughter too. There is time and room for it all.

THE FUNERAL

At about 1:00 p.m. on Friday we loaded into limos and other cars and headed to the church for the funeral. Grandchildren piled in around me and one of them, Grace, climbed right up into my lap for the ride. We got there early so we had an opportunity to meet and greet those who came to celebrate Ned's life with us that day.

Ned was ordained clergy and Fr. Steve did not know what to expect so he cordoned off several rows for clergy. The fact is the clergy who came were the ones we wanted there with us to celebrate his life and ministry – the priests he worked with over the years of his ministry and a few of the Deacons he was close to. They mattered and they came. The Bishop let me know later that on the day of Ned's funeral he said Mass for Ned in his private chapel. That was absolutely the right thing for him to do. It was respectful of the 25 years of ministry Ned gave and yet also honored the needs of his family to be cared for that day by those who provided that daily, ongoing spiritual support to him and to us. Those who came, and those who did not, did the right thing for Ned and for us. This service was about Ned's life and legacy – not the Church. That is what was important to me and what would have mattered most to Ned.

Our family is big and filled with talented musicians, so half the Church was reserved for us and the music was uplifting and powerful. The service was a truly remarkable musical expression of God's love for all of us and the joy of the Resurrection.

I was stunned that the Church was so full and that so many people came such a great distance on really short notice to be there with us. Some people drove 10 to 12 hours round trip on that day to pay their respects and to support us at a challenging and difficult time. I was moved beyond measure to see the outpouring of support. Since that day, I make time to go to the funerals of people I know. That day taught me how much it means to the family to see those faces and to realize that others share their sadness and are there for support and care.

The service was a celebration of life. I am so grateful for all of my big, loving, supportive family members who were there. Some of my friends commented later that when they saw half the church reserved for family, they were a little skeptical. Then we all started arriving and they realized that this was a family gathering and they were the ones invited to join us.

We began with our adult kids covering the casket with the white cloth that covers all caskets that enter a Catholic church for the funeral. When I say "our kids" I mean all our kids - as my friend says - both the born-ins and the marry-ins. Then we followed Ned's casket to the front of the church. I carried the Book of the Gospel that was given him by the Bishop at his ordination. The grandchildren each carried a model train car, which they assembled at the front of the Church.

As I said, we are a family full of musicians so there was no shortage of musical, prayerful magic in the air throughout the service. As I am a musician as well, this was very important to me. It was also important that the service be a joyful celebration of life. Losing him was painful beyond measure but knowing he was now restored and pain-free and no longer bound by the body that betrayed him those last four years was a blessing to all of us.

My older grandchildren, Kathlena and Ethan, had a particularly hard time. They were heartbroken and the service was hard for them. They hugged and held me the whole time. It seemed as if they were afraid to let go of me in case I might disappear too. Ned was a wonderful grandfather – and these two had a special bond with him.

Ned was a model train enthusiast from the time he was 10 years old and he passed on that love of model trains to Ethan, by the time E-Man (Ethan's nickname) was five or six years old.

Ned and Ethan communicated in a kind of shorthand while they worked on model trains. Ned would be working on his layout in Tulsa and Ethan on his layout in Missouri. I remember getting phone calls from 10-year-old Ethan, asking to speak to his Papa. A few seconds later I would notice that the call was over. Ethan just got stuck and, in a few words, Ned told him what to do to move on. No wasted words and no long explanations needed - a grandson and his 68-year old

Papa talking trains. It was a very special bond. The day of the funeral, this ten-year-old handed out the train cars when the grandchildren were lined up in the right order so the train would be "right" at the front of the church and then he supervised putting it together as the children came forward.

At the Peace Greeting, Fr. Steve came over to give us all a hug and asked me if I opened the Book of the Gospel to a particular page when I put it on the casket. I said "No." I had just laid it up there and opened it to lay flat on the top of Ned's casket. Fr. Steve showed me that it was open to the Christmas Gospel.

Now, that might not seem significant to you, but one of the stories we told Fr. Steve was about Ned and the fact that he looked like Santa – or he looked like Tim Allen in the movie "The Santa Clause" and, when Ned grew his winter beard, he was often mistaken by children who saw the movie as that character.

In earlier years when we lived in Enid, Oklahoma, at the Christmas Eve Children's Mass, Ned, dressed as Santa, would come in just as Mass was completing and bring a live baby up the center aisle and lay the baby in the empty manger. He would then kneel and pray at the manger. He would then leave the church waving and saying "Merry Christmas" to all the children and he would be gone before they left Mass. The kids started to really get the connection between Jesus and Santa Claus, and Ned loved making that happen. Fr. Steve saw the fact the book had fallen open to that page as another reminder of Ned's presence among us as we celebrated his life.

Our three adult children had decided they wanted to say something at the end of the service. So, they sat down the day before to talk about how that might go. Shannon is the "writer" in the group so once they made this decision, they put her to work. She says that within about 30 minutes she wrote a poem they called "The Things Dad Taught Us." It is an expression of who he was for them, his humor, his innovation, and his love for me that they experienced and witnessed throughout their lives. The three of them agreed it was the perfect way to complete the service.

Now, for the service, Erica and Shannon knew that taking off their shoes and going up front barefooted was something that would make Ned laugh so they forced Ted to join them in shedding their shoes. They did just that, and from the front of the Church, they read the poem for all of us.

Years later, Erica made us all a poster to remember this poem and the special things they shared about their Dad. It says, in white letters on a red background (which I love as a die-hard Oklahoma Sooner football fan, and he would not have been in favor of):

- *You can build anything and fix it with duct tape.*
- *Hold hands.*
- *Love someone and love them forever.*
- *Everything has a place and that place has a label.*
- *Trust God.*
- *You can smile without ever showing your teeth.*

- *Family is more than just the people who are related to you.*
- *Wear safety goggles.*
- *Mow barefooted.*
- *And finally: CLOTHING IS OPTIONAL.*

As we left the Church and headed to the cemetery, I suddenly realized that we did not give people a map to the cemetery or a way to get to my house after that.

In fact, we had nothing planned at home. I was so focused on the service and what it was going to take to bury him, I forgot about being a hostess. When we got home there was a big tray of sandwiches in the kitchen that one of our neighbors sent over. I was really grateful for their generosity and thoughtfulness.

The cemetery service was hard. The flag on the coffin was startling. I was present to the number of times I have attended funerals and stood nearby the tent listening to the words of interment. Now I was seated in the front row center. No one was between me and the box that would serve as the final resting place for Ned's remains for eternity.

The grandchildren filled up my lap and all the seats around me. They asked a hundred questions which were at once wonderful and difficult. I knew they needed me to be there for them and that they really only understood what they were feeling. They could not see that Grammy was saying goodbye to the love of her life for the last time. I remember Gracie getting off my lap as the officer knelt on one knee in front of me and I heard the words "On behalf of the President of the United States, the Department of the Air Force, and a grateful nation, we offer this flag for the faithful and dedicated service of Edward C. Doty, II".

I guess I never knew that was what was said when the flag was being delivered to the survivors because it took my breath away. I could hardly take the flag from his hands. The finality of that moment was stunning and unexpected. Since that day every time I see a representative of the military drop on one knee in front of a family member to deliver that flag, I hear those words once again.

Signposts:

For the Widow:

Remember that this service is an expression of you, your family and your loved one. Give yourself what you need to celebrate the life and honor the death.

Be grateful for friends and family that surround you and, once again, take care of you.

THE REMAINS

All my life I have heard people use what I considered to be euphemisms to describe the body of the deceased being laid to rest in a cemetery. They spoke of "remains" and "the deceased's body" and said things like "laid to rest" and "final resting place."

Before Ned's death, those were just words to me. Visiting cemeteries was really not my thing. For me it was really clear that the person was no longer there, and I didn't have to go there to be with my memories, love, and thoughts about the deceased. My faith tells me that the soul is gone to the next life and nothing is there but the body so until I buried Ned, I really did not see the need to visit gravesites.

On that day, I got a whole new perspective.

The cemetery on 91st street in Tulsa was just a cemetery. It was beautiful and wooded and the roads were winding and narrow. I noticed it when I drove by and had attended services there for others in years past - but I never really thought about it as anything other than a cemetery – a place where the dead were buried.

However, that day, this same cemetery became the resting place for Ned's remains. In that moment, I got a whole new relationship to what people meant when they referred to "the remains." I really get that what remains here on earth of the man who was a significant part of my life for over 50 years is buried on the hill in the Garden of the Last Supper near the bench and the tree at Calvary Cemetery.

Before I moved away from Tulsa, I would sometimes take my big dog Boomer and just go sit on the bench, near the marker. Maybe I would take a book and read and maybe I would just talk to Boomer and Ned about what was happening in my life. Sometimes I still make the trip back and just go alone and sit. One day I may put another bench there to complete the circle around the tree.

Somehow there is a comfort in knowing that his remains are there. I know it is not him and yet, it is definitely his "remains." It is all I have left of him in this world and it is somehow comforting to know that his remains are there forever.

Since that realization I have a new perspective on the cemetery. When I go back to my hometown, to the place where my parents are buried, I often visit their graves. Just looking at the headstones reminds me of the years of laughter, tears, joy, and pain that were my life with those two amazing human beings. I am reminded of the life lessons they taught me and the fact that my mother wanted to be buried in that area because it overlooked the golf course she loved to play. Her remains are there beside my father – together in death as they were in life – and that too is comforting. It's just the way they would want it to be.

My plan is to be cremated and my kids have specific instructions about the ashes. However, my son has assured me that he will make sure that some of them are right there where his Dad is buried so that our remains left on this earth are also side by side forever.

Signpost:

For the Widow and for Others Experiencing Loss:

Do what gives you peace and comfort with your memories. Each of us needs something different. Don't worry if what you need or what you do does not fit someone else's idea of the thing you "should" need or do.

THE EMPTY HOUSE

The day after the funeral, the kids and I spent several hours together starting to go through Ned's things.

I wanted the kids to have the things of his that mattered to them. Erica and granddaughter, Kathlena, wanted his drawing boards and Ted went through the knives and other items. By the middle of the afternoon I was confronting that this was a new reality and I needed to start dealing with life in this house without him.

While my daughter Erica and I were standing in the kitchen she noticed that something was different with me. She knew instinctively what I needed to hear and said, "Mom, you know that you can tell us to go home. It's okay."

I was so grateful for those words.

I did not want them to feel that I was running them off and, at the same time, I knew that part of the reason I was hanging on to them all being there was to postpone the inevitable impact of being in the house alone – permanently. Her words let me know that my children wanted me to have the space to do what I had to do in my own time.

By late afternoon, I sent everyone home. I knew it was time and so did they. We could not postpone discovering the new normal in our lives.

For the first few minutes after the last of my children and their families headed back to their homes, I just stood in the living room and listened to the silence in the house. The volume of conversation, grandchildren playing, and people coming in and out between Wednesday and Saturday was suddenly gone and it was replaced by a quiet that echoed throughout the house. I breathed deeply and took in the noiseless atmosphere and exhaling, I let go of all the tension that had apparently built up over the last few days in anticipation of this moment. It would be okay. I had been home alone before.

After they were all gone, the kitchen was cleaned, and the house was put back in order, I sat down in my chair in the living room. Within a minute I looked down and saw that I was surrounded by dogs. Lucy, the Golden Retriever, was curled up by my chair and Teddy, my Cavalier King Charles Spaniel was resting on top of my feet.

The house was eerily quiet and as darkness filled the windows, I began to realize that for the first time in my 67 years, I was now living alone.

That is a somewhat startling revelation and one I had never thought about until that moment. As a baby I went home from the hospital with my parents. I moved in with roommates all through college and got married four days after the end of my senior year. Here I was now in a 3,500 square foot house built in 1919 on a third of an acre of land in downtown Tulsa and there was only me and two dogs. The problem was not that there was no one else here. The problem was that Ned's life and aliveness were no longer here.

It did not take long to realize that I was now living in Ned's house.

He was an architect and he loved old houses. Renovating and restoring old houses was a particular gift of his which is why we lived in a house that still had its original gravity air heating system, cove ceilings with a picture rail, lathe and plaster walls in many of the rooms and narrow pine hardwood floors.

He was everywhere in the house. In some ways it was comforting and in other ways it was a reminder of the loss. He was gone and at the same time that he filled every corner of the house, his life and aliveness were conspicuously absent.

That Saturday night was the beginning of a new phase of life for me. No matter how much I would grieve in the next days, weeks, months, and years, the shock of confronting that I was living alone for the first time in my life and that I had no idea how to do that was earthshaking.

One of my oldest and dearest friends said to me the next week that she could not imagine what it was like to be where I was, and my answer was that she was correct. It was one of the most insightful comments anyone made.

Ned had lots of health issues as an adult. As a result, I had often wondered what life would be like if he died. I could not imagine it then and now that I was actually dealing with that reality, I had no idea what was coming. This was totally foreign territory. I never could

have imagined what being a widow would mean or look like on a daily basis.

Since his death, I have come to realize that there is no way to imagine what it is like to be a widow in this society until you are one. However, that Saturday night in March of 2011 I was about to begin a journey into that world. A journey that would lead me to new experiences, provide me with new challenges, open new doors, and close others.

Widowhood is an undistinguished cultural phenomenon in our society.

We don't know it exists until we are thrust into it and those on the outside can have empathy or sympathy for what a widow is experiencing but only another widow really gets it. There are many things about loss that are common experiences for us. However, widowhood is not a common experience that others can imagine any more than the loss of a child or parent is something that can be imagined by one who has never had that experience.

We can be compassionate and sympathetic. We can try to understand the pain and grief but each loss is unique and yet, as someone who has lost both parents,

all my grandparents, best friends, and aunts and uncles, I can tell you that while there are common elements to dealing with loss, the cultural phenomenon encountered by a widow is unique.

Sharing about the challenges and obstacles of that culture, I am hopeful, will let others know that they are not alone on the journey and will begin to open the eyes of society to a way of interacting with women whose spouses have died that is as truly supportive as most want and intend it to be.

Signpost:

For the Widow:

Give yourself time to find a new normal for life. Don't expect too much in the beginning. Just let yourself deal with this new reality at a pace that works for you.

THE NEXT LOSS - OUR LUCY LOU

He called her Lucy Lou and she was supposed to be my dog, but she became Ned's the day we came home from the hospital after his stroke.

Lucy Lou took on caring for him from the very moment we brought him into the house that Thursday until the night he died. That is what Golden Retrievers do.

In fact, we learned this in the first few minutes Ned was back in the house after his stroke. While Ned was hospitalized, the kids, my nephews, and some friends and I moved our bedroom from the large master space upstairs to a smaller bedroom on the main floor. Ned was in a wheelchair now and being on the first floor was easier for both of us. It would also be the best opportunity for him to build his strength and begin to recover his ability to care for himself.

When we got to the house, the first task we had was to get him from the chair to the bed in our new bedroom. We practiced that with the physical therapist at the hospital and were confident we could do this. The problem was that we did not count on a 90-pound Golden Retriever deciding she should help.

In the downstairs bedroom, the space between the wall and the bed was wide enough for the wheelchair to fit comfortably. So, I went in first to the head of the bed and Ned wheeled in behind me so that, with my help, he could stand and turn and sit down on the bed. As I was wedged between the chair and the bedside table and the closet door, assisting Ned in standing and turning, Lucy Lou came bounding over the bed and plopped herself between me and Ned and the chair. Ned and I burst out laughing so hard we could not move. Lucy was also not moving. She was clearly there to help and none of us could move anywhere.

It took a few minutes for us to compose ourselves and figure out a way to move forward. We just had to keep going with a big dog between us until we succeeded in moving Ned from chair to bed.

Once Ned was settled, Lucy went around to my side of the bed and crawled in bed with him and cuddled down beside him. That's when she and I had to have a "Come to Jesus" conversation about where she was going to sleep – and it was not on my side of our bed.

She was Ned's buddy and his faithful companion from that day forward. She went everywhere with him in the house and outside on the deck or in the yard. If he went to take a shower, she sat outside the door until he came out. If he was in the kitchen, she was sitting at his feet. If he went somewhere with me or left to go to physical therapy, she waited by the front door for his return. She spent her days with him, and they had games and activities they did together that helped him regain his movement. They shared snacks (lemon sandwich cookies) every afternoon and he fed her parts of whatever he was eating. This was their relationship until the night he died.

This beautiful dog began grieving the moment he fell over on the bed, dead. Even before the first responders arrived, she knew he was gone, and she curled up in a corner of the kitchen breakfast nook and would not come out to eat or drink that day. When I went to see her before I left with Ted to go to the hospital behind the ambulance, she simply looked up at me for a second with her big sad eyes and then dropped her head back on her paws and slumped further down into the corner. She was heartbroken and she did not know what to do.

The next weeks and days were hard for her – perhaps as hard as they were for the rest of us. She was lost and alone and no amount of cuddling and tempting her with treats could raise her spirits.

Watching her give up after he died was heartbreaking, but in some ways not surprising.

Since the day he came home from the hospital after his stroke four years earlier, she "put" him to bed every night and once he was settled in, she came to let me know he was in bed and he was fine. If I was working in my office upstairs, she came up and put her head in my lap and sat by me for about a minute. Then she went back down to our room and slept on the floor beside him until I came to bed. After I was settled in for the night, she went to her own bed. She was his constant companion for over four years. The night he died, she was devastated and alone and nothing could console her.

On the day of the funeral, when we got home from the cemetery, I was standing in the kitchen talking to someone who came by to pay his respects. I looked out into the dining room and Lucy was standing lengthwise under the glass-topped dining room table with her head in his chair and had the saddest look in her eyes that I have ever seen. She loved him and cared for him and she could not handle losing him.

About four weeks later, she stopped eating and drinking altogether. I tried enticing her with all her favorite things, but she just looked at me and walked away.

A week later she went outside on Sunday morning and never came back in.

Although I knew she was in the back yard, I could not find her anywhere. I called Ted to come help me find her. We located her hidden in a corner of the yard, behind the red caboose storage shed. She clearly went there to die and would not come out no matter what we did or said.

Leslie was there and she and Ted and I cried and cried as Ted crawled back where she was and put her on a big tarp so we could carry her out from behind the caboose. I could not let her suffer any longer. The three of us lifted her into the kids' wagon and loaded her into Ted's truck for a final ride as we headed to the vet.

We knew this was her last journey in this world and we sobbed all the way there. We were losing one more piece of Ned's life and it was harder than I could ever have imagined.

When we met with the vet that Sunday afternoon, she told us that Lucy was barely alive. She asked if we wanted to go with her to the back to complete her journey. I simply could not go back and watch her die and neither could Ted. It was too soon for us to be with someone during that transition again. We said our goodbyes, hugged her a lot and then let her go with the vet.

A few minutes later as we sat in the waiting room, the vet came out and asked if we were Lucy's people. Ted and I looked at each other and smiled and told her "No, "Lucy's people" died a few weeks ago." She then told us that now Lucy had gone to be with her people.

It was a loss we had not expected but were not really surprised by. She was his caretaker and her person was now gone. She no longer knew how to be here without him, so she didn't stay. I loved her enough to respect her decision.

Once again there was a new emptiness in the house. Now it was just me and a little bit of fluff and cuteness in the form of a recently rescued Cavalier King Charles Spaniel called Teddy in that big house.

Signpost:

For the Widow and Others Experiencing Loss:

If you have animals in your life, love them in their grief too. Let them know how much they matter.

MY FRIENDS

My dear friend Leslie hardly let me out of her sight for the first few hours that March morning. She waited until she knew I was surrounded by family before heading off to work. Making sure that I was cared for seemed to be a mission for her during the next year. I can never repay her for being there to walk by my side the miles it was between 45 years married and living single at 67.

Sometimes that was literally walking, like the day we walked to the Cherry Street market for fresh veggies and lunch at Jason's Deli and other times it was to listen while I talked through the myriad of decisions there were to make that were on Ned's side of the scales for almost 45 years – such as what to do about the lawn service and how to deal with all the left over paint in the cans in the basement.

Sometimes it was to be the voice to my thoughts as on the day she came to lunch the week after the funeral and in the middle of the meal she stopped eating, put down her fork, and said, "Okay, I always thought it was your big personality that filled this house. It's not, is it? It was Ned's house and without him, it is really empty."

I could not have said it better myself – and frankly, although it was what I was feeling, I could not have said it at all. She gave voice to what I had been experiencing ever since everyone went home after the funeral.

Leslie and I also belonged to an amazing group of women known as The Breakfast Club. We started having breakfast together to support one another in what we were up to in life and business and to hold each other accountable to following our dreams. We had breakfast almost every week for over 25 years and were a strong support system for each other. Even though some had moved away or left the group, the core group of five women were always there for one another. The other women from The Breakfast Club were at my house within hours to support me and see what they could do. These women are all still an important part of my life and an amazing support network that I value every day.

Another way that friends can provide support is through sharing their memories. Other women have shared with me the difference it has made – even years later – that their friends and neighbors continue to remember their husband and care for her. The nurturing of a widow by the community that knew her and them is a powerful support system that warms the heart and reminds us that gone is not forgotten. We know that. It is nice to know that others know it, too.

Signpost:

For the Widow and for Others Experiencing Loss:

Let your friends support you in dealing with any kind of loss. Lean on them if you need them and let them lean on you when they are struggling or hurting. Be honest with them and be grateful for their love and support.

Let them know that sharing their memories with you means a great deal and is very affirming. Being reminded of kindnesses experienced, joys shared, projects completed, and challenges overcome together is often comforting and always loving.

THE GRANDCHILDREN - AND ME

During the days following Ned's death, my grandchildren were my sanity. They hugged me often and cried for missing their Papa. They held my hand and made sure I was taken care of.

They asked me odd questions like "Is my Papa died?" and did I think that he would take care of their dog that died a few months earlier now that he died too. That precious little one even asked a friend of Ted and Treasure's if she thought we would get another Papa. You see, her mom and dad told her that after Annie, their dog, died, they could get another dog one day. At age four, it just seemed logical that the same would apply to grandpas who died. Maybe there was a store or a rescue shelter for Papas, too.

They worried about how they would get cookies now because Papa was the cookie distributor in our house. They offered to teach me how so that cookie eating could continue. Then they wanted to know if, now that he was gone, we could get chocolate cookies. They thought he preferred lemon cookies. They did not know that he bought lemon cookies because chocolate was not good for the dog and he and Lucy had a cookie snack every afternoon.

They reminded me that they missed seeing him and told me about the things they did with him that were fun and heartwarming.

Remember that during the funeral procession, the grandchildren each carried a train car. Kathlena, our first grandchild, carried the engine and, as I said, Ethan, our oldest grandson and Ned's model train buddy, took charge of the whole thing. The train on the steps in front of the altar was their idea. They wanted everyone to know all about him.

The grandkids all piled into the limo with me and sat on my lap and each other so we could be together on the trip to the church and the cemetery. They reminded me minute by minute of the joy that a loving family brings to life and the comfort that joy brings in dealing with death. At the cemetery they filled the front row and my lap. Gracie plopped down on my lap and stayed there asking me questions about what was happening as Fr. Steve and the pall bearers finished the service that laid Ned in his final resting place.

The grandchildren asked me to keep the house because for them, it was his house.

In their minds he is forever linked to that stately clinker brick house with the huge backyard that included an amazing playground he built for them – because Kathlena asked him to. The red caboose he built as a storage building in the back yard was just the right touch for their Papa's yard.

When I finally decided to sell the house a few years later, the youngest, Eli, came to talk to me about the house and missing his Papa more when I moved. He was only five at the time and he was worried that if I sold the house and moved, he would forget his Papa. We talked about where his memories were, and he discovered that they would always be with him. The memories belonged to him, not the house. When he left that day, he told me it was okay to let go of the house because he would always have Papa with him.

Signpost:

For the Widow:

"And a little child shall lead them"… If there are children in your life, let them remind you of the simplicity and joy of loving, loss, and precious memories.

KATHLENA

For Kathlena (or Kat as she now prefers), the last four years of Ned's life were very hard. The Papa she knew built play yards in the back, designed circuses, build a big deck, grilled the best chicken and hamburgers on his big Hasty Bake, played with all the grandkids in the pool, and spent endless hours in the basement train room building layouts.

She was the first grandchild and spent lots of time with him from the time she was born. When she could sit up on her own, she had her own chair in the train room where she could watch him create mountains and buildings and build train bridges for those big layouts he was always working on. So, for Kathlena, the stroke was costly in a different way. The Papa she knew – the one that was her best pal -was never the same again. He could not do the things they always did anymore and sometimes he was gruff and grumpy in ways she had never experienced. It was hard for her to see that happen to him and harder still to understand why that happened to her Papa.

It was also hard for me to watch her struggle with his limitations. Kathlena, who was 8 when he had the stroke and 12 when he died, was hit hardest but that's because she had spent the most time with him of any of the grandkids. From the time she was born, she was a regular in our house and spent endless hours with him. They played, colored, took walks, built play yards, swam and did lots of fun things together from the time she was a baby. She spent a good deal of her infancy sleeping in the crook of his knees on his lap in the living room chair.

On her 2nd birthday, she went with him and me to Bristow to watch her dad and her Aunt Erica run in the Flower Run, which was dedicated that year to my mother, who was battling back from a paralyzing injury. Kathlena spent the entire day with Ned and me and most of the time I was in charge of her. I fed her breakfast and lunch and held her hand and carried her during the day. Later we took her home for a nap before her 2-year-old birthday party.

When Ned and I drove up to the house for the party we got out of the car. She was in the front yard waiting dressed in her prettiest outfit. When Ned got out of the car, she started running toward him yelling "Papa! Papa!" As she saw me getting out of the car on the other side, she stopped dead in her tracks and said, (to everyone's laughter) "Who's that?" Even today when we are all together someone will see me come in the room and say, "It's Who's That?"

Such was the relationship between Kathlena and Ned from the day she was born. When the older kids in the family wanted to play with electronic games or trains that were declared by Ned to be off limits, she could be heard telling them that she would go ask – because he would not say "No!" to her. She was right.

Five years after Ned died, Kathlena wrote the most amazing tribute to him and the experience of losing him for a school literature project. Her teacher asked her to share it with her family, so she posted it on Facebook

and we all cried at this moving expression of what it was like for her to lose him first to the stroke and then to the pulmonary embolism that ultimately took his life.

The story is included here as a reminder to us all that we beat ourselves up over and over for the things we don't do that we think we should do and then we think others are upset with us because of it –and that there can be those among us who are suffering in ways we can't see and don't understand.

In this case, Ned's stroke impacted his cognitive ability to connect some of the dots and left him hyper-focused on his own limitations and disabilities. He did not really notice that she was not around as much – not because he did not care but because his brain was not working the same way it always had. He was thrilled when any of the grandchildren came over. However, Kathlena apparently saw her behavior after the stroke as inconsistent with her relationship with him even though she was only 12 when he died and only 8 when he had his stroke. Five years later she confronted this demon she had been living with since his death and wrote this amazing piece about that journey.

I Forgive You

This crisp Autumn breeze combed through her hair as she sat at the red light on 91st and Harvard.

91st and Harvard. It took her 20 minutes to get to this intersection; much longer than she planned. She glanced at the clock: 11:30. Exhaling, she looked up at the still red streetlight, and rested her hands at the top of her steering wheel. This thing insider her, black and gooey and snake-like, she could feel it moving, coiling through her insides. It lightly wiggled through her stomach, coiling itself up within. The urge to vomit rose from this black-gooey-snake-like thing inside of her stomach, considering it couldn't stay still. It kept kicking and writhing within her, and she had to grab her stomach to calm it down.

Green Light.

Deep Breath.

Turn Right.

Welcome to Calvary.

*It had been almost five years since she'd been in this place. It had been almost five years that she had been avoiding this place. It had been almost five years since she's seen **him**, Edward Cunningham Doty II, her grandfather. She had been too scared to pay him a visit, so many doubts, and apologies she had for him. Her hands trembled at the thought of seeing him again, and she almost turned herself around. Sitting there in the parking lot of the office though, she spotted a familiar white Toyota Corolla…**He actually came…?! He's here, oh my God, he's actually here!** A smile spread across her face, and the black snake-like creature within her settled down. He's here, her best friend.*

She had asked him almost a week ago to go see her grandfather with her, since she was too scared to go alone, and he's here, her best friend.

Left Turn.

Parking Lot.

Deep Breath.

Parked.

She hopped out of her truck, and smiled to him, the creature burrowing itself deeper within the pit of her stomach.

"Shall we?" An extended hand, thick black glasses, combed back dirty blonde hair.

"Yes" Grasping his hand tight, a burrowing black creature wanting to escape.

The crisp Autumn breeze blew ever so softly. It was indeed, an incredibly beautiful day, the sun was out, and not a cloud in the sky. The two had decided to walk instead of driving the rest of the way based on this fact. They chatted, the boy and the girl, to lighten the ever so heavy smog that hung in the air around her. She really didn't want to be here, but she needed to- both for an AP paper, and to clear her conscience, and he knew that. If he wasn't here, she wouldn't be here. A black and gooey and snake-like creature coiled within her, wondering what her grandfather would think of him. Good or bad? Who knew?

"So, where exactly is it?"

"Dad did say it was over by the office, so it has to be here somewhere."

Up the Hill.

Deep Breath.

To the Left.

The Passover Section.

She vaguely remembered her dad telling her he'd be under the only tree in the lot. But there were so many trees. So many trees, and so many people, and she couldn't see him. The creature began to writhe within her. **What is we can't find him? O God, no, what if we can't find him?** Her hand was squeezed, and she looked to her best friend.

"Hey. It'll be alright. We'll find him." The creature calmed. The two squeezed into the sea of people. Sliding through, stepping around-there were so many it overwhelmed her. Honestly, she hardly remembered what her grandfather looked like; it had been that long since she had come to visit him. Her mind swarmed as her eyes darted across the sea of people, hoping to recognize him in some way.

Row one.

Row two.

Edward Cunningham Doty II,

August 20th 1943 – March 23rd 2011

"There. That's him."

It was different than she remembered. Before, it was a brown mound of dirt with just a name plate. Now, it was a worn gray piece of stone, with a book engraved on the surface. Oh, he loved books, he

was obsessed with books. It's where her love of books came from. A single tear came to her eye, followed by another, and another, and another. He grabbed her close, her best friend, her grandfather. The black and gooey and snake-like creature died within her, leaving the heaviness of its corpse within the pit of her stomach.

*Her eyes shut, and images barraged her mind. Crisp and clear, foggy and muddy, images of her and her grandfather, **Her Papa.** As a child, he was her best friend. She was his best friend since his wife, my Grammy, was always at work. She spent the majority of her childhood with this man, spending nights, and weekends when her parents were too busy to keep an eye on her. They designed circuses, houses, and a tree house-which he actually built for her. He was an architect, made* her want to be an architect when she was "all grown up." He was a Father, a Deacon, a Papa, disabled. Her Papa was disabled. She couldn't exactly remember when he had his stroke, but she remembered how she treated him differently. Stupid girl, she was afraid of him- afraid of him and his wheelchair. **Stupid girl. Stupid Girl. STUPID GIRL.** Every time she would go to visit him and her grandmother, she avoided him, designing house and circuses with him. The older she got, the more ignorant towards him she got. Not caring or even thinking about that one time they tried to pick all of the seeds off strawberries, or how they would walk Riverside together in the Fall to see the Autumn colors.

Fall. Autumn. It brought her back to her standing place at the base of his grave. She stared at **March 23rd, 2011** remembering that fateful day, the heart attack. **I'm, so sorry...forgive me for my ignorance.**

"It's alright, I got you."

She looked to her best friend and smiled, so thankful he was here, and he smiled back, so thankful he was here. They hugged each other tightly, and she hid her face in his chest.

"It's alright, I forgive you." The corpse of the creature was finally lifted from the pit of her stomach- five years after it was born within her. **Light.**

She smiled in the chest of her best friend, her grandfather.

"Thank you." A soft whisper, only heard by the ears of the dead.

Tears Wiped Away.

A Kiss to the Forehead.

A Goodbye.

Heading Home.

"I forgive you, I forgive you."

Before that visit to the cemetery, Kathlena had been beating herself up for the way she thought she abandoned him after the stroke. That day changed everything. Today she is an amazing artist on her way to a degree in graphic design and more than once she has posted something she created and reminded all of us that his creativity and artistic ability lives on in her. He is still her Papa and will always be the best friend she had as she made her way into this world as a young child.

Signpost:

For the Widow and Others Experiencing Loss:

Remember that we often blame ourselves for things that are not our fault and then we live like that blame is real and true. Let it go and remember the joy and love.

ETHAN

Ethan lived further away so in some ways it was a bit easier for him to deal with the aftermath of the stroke. He did not see Ned often and Papa could still answer the train questions. They just could not work together on the layouts anymore and I know he missed that. He tried so hard to let his Papa know that he was taking up the "model train guy" mantel for him and Ned was proud and pleased to know how much it meant to Ethan to learn from him.

In the summer after Ned died, Ethan came to spend a few days with me, and we sorted the hundreds of train cars that were in Ned's collection. Ethan helped me create a train for each of the children and grandchildren. We discovered 37 HO Gauge engines and over 300 cars plus more than 40 buildings and miles and miles of track. There are still trains in my garage and parts for building layouts in Erica and Chris' basement with Ethan's trains.

He worries more about me. He would call me from time to time just to see what I was doing and to this day he calls and talks to me about lots of things. He asked to come spend the day with me on his 11th birthday and go to an OU game. At the party before the game the host introduced Ethan to about 2,000 fans and wished him "Happy Birthday." He then asked Ethan what he wanted for his birthday and gave Ethan the microphone. Never one to miss an opportunity to speak up, Ethan stood tall in the middle of the table and said that the best thing he could get for his birthday was spending the day with his Grammy at the football game.

A few months later I found out that the Great American Train Show was stopping in Olathe, Kansas, over the Christmas break. No one else in the family wanted to go with Ethan so I drove to Smithville, Missouri to get him and we had a great day together. As we stood in line to go in the show, he was chattering endlessly about nothing – again not an unusual occurrence with Ethan at that age – and then when we went through the door, he got very quiet and his eyes were as big around as saucers. As he walked past the first display, he took my hand and looked up at me and said "Grammy, this day is pure joy." He was totally correct. For me this was both a joy to relive something I had done many times with Ned during our 45 years and boundless joy to see the smile on that young man's face that day.

Three years after Ned died I got a call from Ethan asking me when I was coming to Missouri again. I told him what date I had planned to come, and he asked if he could take me out on a date. Well, I never had a date with an 11-year-old before and it sounded fun. When I got to the house (after a five hour drive) he was waiting outside dressed in his Easter clothes, ready to go. He chose a good restaurant that he liked, and he knew I would enjoy and after dinner we went window shopping at a nearby mall. He was so proud of himself and I was beaming with pride all evening.

He recently lost his other grandfather and it has been really hard for him. Once again, he is concerned for his

Grandma Debbie. He wanted his mom and dad to invite Debbie to come to Branson with them. He was worried that things are too hard for her now. Ethan has a heart of gold and a gift for reaching out to others who might be suffering. I have learned a lot from his compassion and caring. He made many of the transitions to widowhood for me easier. I hope I can do the same for others.

Signpost:

For the Widow and Others Experiencing Loss:

Reaching out with compassion and care can lighten the load for everyone. Look for ways to touch other's lives. It will enrich yours immeasurably.

THE YOUNGER ONES

Hayden, Gracie, and Brianna were younger and mostly they were confused by Ned's stroke. They were young enough to know something happened to him and that he was different but too young to really understand what was going on. Hayden, who was Ethan's age at the time, was closer to me and spent a lot more time with me than with Ned. We did lots of things together and still do. She lived close by, but Gracie lived in Missouri and Brianna lived in Texas and they were three years old at the time of his stroke so most of their enduring memories are of Papa after he got sick.

The youngest of the grandchildren, Maddox, Lachlann, and Eli, only knew the Papa who was in a wheelchair and could not walk without a walker or a cane. Maddox and Lachlann were born in June before his stroke on Labor Day and Eli was born two years later.

The Papa these three knew lived confined to the first floor of the house. He was the cookie distributor in chief and he could be counted on to have those treats available and to handle the distribution anytime they came over. Eli spent many afternoons snuggling in his arms rolling around the first floor in the wheelchair at the end of a nap after two-year-old "school".

The older kids had a hard time dealing with his limitations from the stroke, but the younger ones only knew him that way so for them he was fine in a chair or walking with a cane or walker. It was okay that he could not climb the steps or climb the ladder to the pool or play with them in the yard or take them to the park. They never knew that he could. The older kids could see how much he lost, and it was harder for them to know how to be with the new version of Papa.

A few months after he died Shannon and Brian and the kids were driving down 91st street taking home Brianna's friend who had spent the night. They passed Calvary Cemetery at 91st and Harvard and Shannon heard Bri say to her friend that her Papa was buried there. When the friend asked who that was, Brianna responded "He was a really old man who loved us a lot." How much more could a grandparent ask from an eight-year-old struggling to deal with the death of a loved one?

Signpost:

For Others:

We all leave a legacy. Why not leave the young a legacy of love? We can all do that in many ways.

MY BODY'S RESPONSE

A few days after the funeral, I started to notice some things happening in my body that were a bit frightening. I knew there would be an emotional impact of losing him and that would last a long time, but this was different. This did not have anything to do with losing Ned or my grief. This was physical.

The first thing I noticed was in the shower. When I closed my eyes to shampoo my hair, I lost my balance and fell against the wall. What was that about? Balance problems disappeared when I had my knees replaced a couple of years earlier. At first, I thought it was just a fluke. Maybe it was a onetime occurrence brought on by not drinking enough water or eating enough. After all, eating was not high on my priorities that week.

However, the situation did not improve. Every time I took a shower or closed my eyes for any reason, I started to lose my balance. It happened so often that I started to take extra care to keep from falling in the same way I had before knee surgery.

Then came the realization . . . I could no longer concentrate.

As someone who has always prided herself on being able to keep several balls in the air at the same time and get the jobs done as expected, now I was not able to concentrate on anything for more than 10 minutes without taking a break to get refocused and certainly I could not focus on more than one thing at a time. It was very disconcerting, even scary. If I was working on an article I was writing, for example, after 10 minutes I would lose my train of thought and I had to get up and walk around and do something mundane to allow my brain to refocus and then I could put in 10 more minutes on the article. If the phone rang and someone asked me a question, I would have to stop working, turn my full attention to the question and get present to what was being asked before I could respond - most of the time this was a monumental task.

I was afraid I was losing my mind and that something was really wrong with my body. When I connected all these things together in my mind, the options I came up with were pretty scary. I shared with Leslie that I was worried that I would never be able to concentrate again for any length of time. It was as if I was drifting in and out of life. Sometimes I was there and fully participating and then, very shortly and with no warning, I would be drifting away and unable to concentrate on anything. Then, without warning, I was unbalanced and catching myself to keep from falling.

The fear of what might be happening to me and the realization that my children had just lost their father and could not lose me too, sent me to see my doctor. I remember being in the room waiting and thinking of all the possible things he could say. At the same time, I was praying feverishly that it was not serious. As it turns out he said nothing that I expected him to say and what he said has proven to be incredibly valuable to lots and lots of people through the years.

This doctor had been taking care of me for over 20 years. He knew a lot about me, my family, and my medical history. When he came in the room, I started telling him about all the physical experiences I was having with my balance and my concentration. I told him that my kids had just lost their father and they could not lose me too, so we had to find out what was happening to me. When I stopped long enough to take a breath, he said "Sharon, your husband just died." I said, "I know that, but you don't understand. Now something is terribly wrong with me." He said, again, "Sharon, your husband just died." I could not figure out why he was saying that so, once again I said, "I know, but there is something wrong with me now and I have to find out what it is." Once again, he responded very slowly with "Sharon, your husband just died."

The third time I finally heard what he was saying, and I asked if he was telling me that the things I was experiencing were connected to Ned's death.

His response was to explain to me how the body deals with major trauma or stressors. He said when our body deals with things like the death of a spouse or parent, chemicals are released in the body that take a long time to dissipate and require a lot of the body's resources to deal with. He said that what I was experiencing was normal and that for the time being the most important thing there was to do was get plenty of rest and slow down. He suggested I take some of the responsibilities I had off my plate for a while and turn them over to someone else. He recommended that I read a good book, take daily walks, take a nap and generally take it easy for a while and – most important – take folic acid. He said that folic acid could help the body deal with the trauma induced chemical dump. My body was now reacting to Ned's death and that was totally unexpected – and comforting. After all, I was not dying of some horrible disease – I just needed to slow down and let my body heal itself.

I left the office mystified by how my body got me through the first days after his death and how it was now dealing with the entire trauma and I was grateful that was all it was. Now, I also had some mild symptoms of depression, which the doctor also said was normal, but we agreed that, unless they worsened, I would do what I knew to do to get through that temporary situation without medication.

When I got home, I sent an email to the kids. I told them about my recent experiences, the fears I had about what was happening to me and everything the doctor said about it. They all contacted me and thanked me for letting them know. It seems they were dealing with something similar and were also fearful that it was something wrong with them. Turns out we were all able to breathe a sigh of relief that day – and then head to the store and get folic acid.

I know that many others experience depression that requires medication to get through and when I tell others about my doctor's recommendation about folic acid, I suggest they check with their own doctor to see if that might help them concentrate. I'm not a doctor. I just know what helped was finding out that there was a simple answer to what I was experiencing and something I could do to help my body heal from the trauma.

I was lucky I was able to turn the depression around without taking any other medications. There are times when the same feelings and emotions set in again but now I can see it coming and sometimes I know when to look out for it - like during the week between Christmas and New Year's. When I know what to expect, I can take action quickly to turn the tide.

Our body is an amazing machine. It takes over and provides what we need to deal with the major traumas that life hands us. We just don't always know that it also takes time to recover physically from those traumas. After all my body was not hurt by Ned's death - or at least that is what I thought. Turns out I was really wrong about that – and since my children experienced some of the same emotions and physical reactions, this part of the process is not just about being a widow. It is about experiencing profound loss.

Signpost:

For the Widow and For Others Experiencing Loss:

Pay attention to your body. Listen to what it is saying to you as you deal with loss. Ask your doctor about adding folic acid to your diet as you recover. Remember that your whole body experiences traumatic loss.

"PITY THE POOR WIDOW"

This sentiment is an undercurrent in many of our responses to women who lose their husbands to death.

It is not something that people are aware of and yet it permeates almost every aspect of how society relates to and interacts with widows. It is like a sub-culture of our society that is hidden from view until you are thrust into it by the death of your husband. Virtually every widow I have spoken to about this has had the same experience of suddenly being in a different reality called "widow" and being confronted with new rules for behavior, new expectations for how you should respond, and new ways that society, including your friends and family, see you and deal with you.

The first few days I was really just dealing with the reality of being alone and I was just getting a glimpse of how much had changed in an instant. Everything was different. It wasn't just about being alone. It was about everything. There was less laundry to do and fewer dishes to wash. There were fewer groceries to buy and no one but me to cook for. There was no one to call to let them know I would be later than expected getting home. These are the kind of things that become obvious right away.

However, the first time I was really present to this new cultural world I had entered was when I went to an event at my Church the week after Ned's funeral. I had been attending events by myself for some time as my husband's physical challenges after his stroke substantially limited his activities, particularly evening outings. Couple that with the fact that at heart he was somewhat of a hermit and he saw the stroke as a justification for staying home from public events the last few years he was alive. You can see that I was often attending events by myself. Something was very different now, however. I wasn't just going to things by myself because he could not or did not want to go. I was alone at events because I was alone.

When I walked into the Parish Hall that night, I was immediately met by our wonderful, thoughtful priest and escorted to a table where several other women were already seated. He introduced me to the other women with these words, "You probably know Sharon, but you may not know that she too is a widow now. Her husband was buried last Friday."

It seems that all the women at that table were widows. I was now officially part of that group. I was a widow and I was seated at the "widow's table!" Just two weeks before that, I came to a similar event and found my own place at a table among my friends from choir. Now I was expected to sit among the widows of the parish at the table set aside for them.

One of the most disturbing things about this for me was that although I was the past President of the Parish Council and a longtime member of the community, I had no idea this table even existed. It was a jolt to realize that this group of women was essentially marginalized and set aside, and no one recognized what was happening. In fact, the "widows" related to the whole experience as thoughtful and caring.

Very quickly that night I was introduced to some of the unique aspects of the world at the widow's table. First, the conversation was all about widowhood and how stunned they were that I was already out of the house and re-engaging in life. One woman even said to me that she could not even get off the couch for about four years after her husband's death. She followed that with an explanation (out loud but clearly to herself) that, of course, her situation was different because her husband had health problems and she had to be his caregiver for four years before he died. I did not have the heart to tell her that the same was true for me. She needed to justify to herself why she was immobilized by his death and trapped in her own home without engaging in life for so long after he was gone and here I was at a Church supper a week after Ned's funeral.

One of the interesting things I learned that night about widows, particularly those, like me, who were of a certain age and no longer had children at home, was that the biggest thing they had to deal with was what to do with their life without "him." After all, like me they don't have children at home to demand that we get back in action right away. We had lives, and sometimes very long lives, that were woven together with the wishes, hopes, dreams, and actions of our husbands – and now he and that life are gone. Many of us also dealt with long illnesses that consumed our thoughts and actions for months or even years.

Younger widows with children may be confronting the same loss but they don't seem to have the luxury of dealing with it slowly or dwelling in the loss. There are so many demands on them around their children that they have to get back in action as soon as possible. It certainly does not make the journey any easier or any less traumatic, but it does provoke activity and sometimes that can give you a different perspective. It can, I am told, take your mind off yourself and your situation momentarily from time to time at least.

As someone who had more than 50 years of life that included him in its very fabric but did not depend on him for its existence, that part of the process was less challenging for me. We were married almost 45 years and shared all our hopes, dreams, and wishes. He was dealing with the aftermath of a massive stroke for almost four years before he died and that stroke dramatically changed my life. Four years before he died, I became his caregiver. However, I was also independent and active in my consulting business and part of my life did not change so much. I traveled less those last four years, but my office was at home, so my other work continued and in that world, I was not a "widow". I was the same person I was before he died.

What was difficult was being relegated to the status of "widow." I was now suddenly not welcome at "couples" events and almost all the couples Ned and I socialized with no longer even called. I was now dining alone at home and out – not by choice but because I was alone. I was now expected to join the other widows at events and activities and if I was invited to an activity or social event that was primarily couples, I was left to fend for myself as the third wheel.

This was true even when I went to events I had gone to alone for years. Things were different now. It was not acceptable for me to continue to be friends with men in our circle who were widowers or divorced – even if I had no interest in a relationship other than friendship. It was no longer okay to be friendly because now I was a widow!

The conversation around me changed dramatically. A couple of times I thought of that old comment many mothers have made that until they were pregnant, they never noticed other pregnant women but as soon as they got the news, it seemed there were pregnant women everywhere.

For me it now seemed that everywhere I went I was surrounded by widows. Maybe they were there all along and I just never paid attention to them being a "widow" or maybe I was now being steered in that direction by others such as the priest at my parish. Perhaps what I was just now seeing was society's way of defining me by my marital status.

Regardless of why it was happening, there I was in the midst of a world of widows. Their conversation was predictable. They wanted to know how long I was married; how long ago he died, what happened to him, and do I have children and grandchildren. Not once did one of them ask me what I did for a living. Not once was I asked about my professional or volunteer activities and, if that subject came up, they either changed the subject or left the conversation.

The newly discovered widows in my world had lives that seemed to be centered on what happened before "he" died and how they dealt with his death. They took trips together. They shopped together. They had lunch together and they visited the cemetery together.

They are lovely women and I know they were coping in the way they knew best, but this was not my path. I went to lunch with a large group of them from my parish once and was asked if I wanted to join a new ministry at the church to provide care and comfort to widows.

Everywhere I turned I was confronted by society's idea that the loss of my husband put me in a special category of human being. Without my permission or input, on the day he died I was relegated to that domain called "widowhood" and everyone but me seemed to know what that was supposed to be like, how I was supposed to now act, and what I was expected to tolerate from others.

My experience is that for the rest of the world the widow is to be pitied – after all, her husband died, and he was the real center of her life. What will she do now without that center sustaining her? Her value is also much less because he is no longer there to maintain their status as a couple.

Many widows seemed to think that women of a certain age should just follow the rules and do widowhood the way it was meant to be done. The expectation of the rest of the world seems to be that we take a back seat to life, be glad we had the time we had, and spend the rest of our days trying to find a way to live without our husbands – or looking for a new one.

Being thrust into this world view was startling for someone as independent and self-sufficient as me and I have since learned that other women have a similar response. I have a thriving consulting business and an active life of community service. I lead workshops and give presentations all over the country in my field and I go wherever I want to go and do whatever I want to do. I have season tickets to OU football and never miss a game. I've been known to drive 5 hours round trip to attend a grandchild's school program, theatre production, or baseball game. This year alone I have been to England, Ireland, and Scotland, traveled to Atlanta to help my children get settled in their new house, reinvented a major fundraiser for local charities in my community, and put about 45,000 miles on my car going to see children, grandchildren, and friends. My husband died in 2011 – I did not!

That first Friday night after Ned's funeral, I began to see what I was now dealing with in reality. "Pity the poor widow" was not just some saying, it was the way the world saw "widow." Other people in my life kept directing me to these groups of what I call "widowomen." I was now one of them – a widow - and with that label came a long list of expectations that were hidden from view until that moment. Society has it all figured out. Widows are just expected to go along.

Signpost:

For Others:

Notice how you see the women in your life who are dealing with this loss. See them as people – not widows. See them as women – not widows. See them has creative, giving, caring, human beings – not widows. And remember they are learning how to live a new life – not how to live with a death.

"I'M SORRY FOR YOUR LOSS"

Another aspect of that "widowoman" culture is that people that were friends and acquaintances for years now did not seem to know what to say to you other than "I am sorry for your loss" and "How are you doing?"

At the funeral and in the days after he died it was expected. People were genuinely sorry that Ned died and everyone around me was concerned about how I was dealing with the shock of his death. However, several years after Ned's death people still stop conversations to let me know they are sorry for my loss and wonder how I am doing. Others have shared the same experience with me and that after a while it no longer occurs like a real expression of sympathy.

In fact, these days it happens at the strangest times and under what seems to me to be unusual circumstances. I will be having a conversation with someone about something that has nothing to do with loss and I make some reference to Ned having died a few years ago – often to point to some time frame. Suddenly the other person will stop the conversation to make sure I hear them say how sorry they are for my loss – even if the comment is untimely and not really appropriate in the circumstances.

This phenomenon is not limited to "widows." It seems that virtually everyone who suffers the loss of an important person in their life has a similar experience.

My children have all dealt with being reactivated by the phrase "I'm so sorry for your loss." Once my son called me once and said, "If one more person says to me that they are sorry for my loss, I am going to deck them."

For my children, however, these automatic expressions of sorrow stopped almost entirely after the first year. For widowomen that is not the case. No matter how long ago he died, a widow is still hearing that people are sorry for her loss and wondering how she is doing for years to come. The experience of dealing with that phrase and questions about how I am doing over and over and over again for years after Ned's death has made me realize that the conversation is almost as automatic as breathing. It's similar to the "How are you?" that begins every conversation and the "I'm fine" said thoughtlessly in response.

Some have found a way to deal with it that is unique and self-nurturing. My friend Terry Gobbo, a young widow with children who made such a big difference for me in the first weeks and months after Ned's death, shared with me that she got really tired of people saying "Sorry for your loss" and then asking how she was when she knew they really were only asking out of obligation. She did not want to hurt anyone else's feelings or to be rude, so, she decided to find a way to respond with integrity.

She knew that "Fine" was what people wanted to hear when they inquired about how she was doing. They did not really want to know what she was dealing with. They just wanted to satisfy themselves that she was fine and feel good about asking her. So, she decided that for her FINE was an acronym for Frustrated, Insecure, Neurotic, and Exhausted. When she answered people who asked how she was she could say "Fine" without feeling like she was lying. It allowed her to both express herself honestly and to satisfy the needs of the other person in one word – and really mean what she said.

People don't know what to say and they are convinced that they should say something. They want you to know they realize you suffered a loss and that it must be painful. They have heard others say they are sorry for the loss and it seems like the right thing to say. They hear it on television. They see it on Facebook and social media. They have heard their parents and other adults in their lives say it for years. "I am so sorry for your loss" seems to be the right thing to say because everybody does it. The problem is that when it is an automatic response that too is apparent and as an automatic response it does not communicate any of the compassion or empathy people think they are expressing.

This particular issue seems to be difficult for people to understand and accept. At times I have shared my frustration about this automatic reaction with others and the response has been interesting. Without exception, others have told me that I am wrong to think the way that I do. They have stressed that regardless of how I hear it, taking the time to say they are sorry for the loss is a sensitive and thoughtful thing to do. Some have told me that my reaction is inappropriate and just plain off and that instead, I should be grateful that others care and take the time to express their concern.

This reaction to my comments left me with feeling that these expressions of automatic concern for another's loss are more about them feeling better about how they are responding than truly expressing a concern for the one dealing with the loss.

I am also convinced that they are sure that the expression of sorrow is something people really do want to hear and should be grateful for. The problem is that none of that has anything to do with the person dealing with the loss. It's all about the good intentions of the person saying they are sorry for your loss.

Those who want to make a real difference for someone dealing with this kind of loss can do so by simply listening to what they are saying, being present with the person and responding accordingly.

Let go of the auto response. If something needs to be said, say words that let her know that you were listening and paying attention to what she was saying and feeling. The comments that meant the most to me were those that let me know the other person was genuinely interested in what I was dealing with and was really listening to what I had to say.

Signpost:

For Others:

Listen and respond to what's being said. Expressing sympathy or empathy because you "should" makes no difference.

A MORE "PERSONAL" RESPONSE

Introducing someone as a widow provokes an almost predictable response after a while. Widows begin to recognize the reaction. Most people are compassionate and caring and are genuinely concerned for the woman in front of them that is dealing with a loss they can only imagine. Others – not so much. I had many experiences of both kinds. Some are demonstrations of what NOT to do and others show real thoughtful, caring, compassion for someone dealing with the loss of a loved one.

One example of what NOT to do cost me a doctor whose care I appreciated and needed. After our interaction I was just not willing to go back there again. It also reminded me that some people don't have a clue how to be with others without always and only forwarding their own agenda and concerns.

So, here is what happened.

About two weeks after Ned died, I had an appointment with my chiropractor. Over the years I had noticed that the office atmosphere was more and more faith based in every respect. There was only Christian music playing in the background. There were only Christian inspired magazines in the waiting room, and everyone was always "blessed" on their way into the treatment room and their way out the front door.

Now, my Christian faith is the bedrock of my life, so this emphasis on Christian atmosphere was fine with me as the culture of my doctor's office. However, on the day of this appointment I realized that this was more than a Christian environment. It was also an opportunity for the doctor to proselytize. It was his chance to preach to me and lead me through this experience – his own way, with or without my permission.

There were about 10 people in the waiting room when he came over to get me and asked what had been happening in my life. I told him that Ned died two weeks earlier and that's what I was dealing with.

His response was not the compassion and concern I had come to expect. The first words out of his mouth were, "Did he know Jesus?" I was taken aback at the question. He had turned to face me and put his hands on my arms, held me in place and asked the question without one word to me about what I was dealing with or even how it might be affecting my body.

I answered with a stunned "Yes" and then he started giving me a sermon about how God would take care of me and that God was my husband now. He was also holding my arms down to my side and I was backed up to a chair and felt trapped. Remember we are standing in the waiting room during all this and he is going on and on quoting scripture about how God is going to step in and step up to fill in my needs like a husband. I let him talk and said nothing in return until we were in the exam room and he was continuing to go on and on about God being my husband. I just wanted my spine aligned but that was not all he was providing that day.

Well, God is my rock and my foundation, but God is not my husband and never will be. The doctor kept up this "sermon" during the entire treatment and I just listened and, frankly, got more and more annoyed. By the time my adjustment was complete I was completely done with the "Sermon in the Exam Room" and the pompous arrogance of this man. So, as he said, one last time, "you are so privileged to have God as your husband now and for eternity", I turned and with a big smile on my face I said: "Well, if God is my husband, he better step it up because the yard work is not getting done!" I walked out of the office and never went back.

In that interaction and a few others over the years, I realized that there are people who cannot see outside their own agenda. They think they have an answer for you, and you should be grateful for their input – even if you don't have their same question or concern they want to answer.

Now, this situation is not unique to widowhood. However, it is not always as blatantly apparent as it was on this day.

It reminded me of how focused we often are on our own agenda, our own needs, and what we think is most important. One of my favorite quotes about communication is from George Bernard Shaw, who said: "The single greatest problem in communication is the illusion that it has taken place."

Hopefully one of the things I am taking away from this journey is a renewed commitment to listening and being with others in such a way that they know I am there for and with them regardless of what is going on in my life or my head.

In addition to the situations that were challenging and difficult, there were other responses that moved and touched me profoundly.

My sister-in-law, Paulette, came by my house about a week after the funeral and brought me a book. She told me that some friends had recommended it to her and said it made a real difference for them when they lost a loved one. She wanted me to have "Heaven is for Real" so that when I was ready I could read it and perhaps be comforted by the story. It took me a few months to read it, but she was right. It was a thoughtful, caring thing to do and I was truly moved by the message of the book and the comfort it brought me.

Another friend subscribed to a series of pamphlets for me about grief and loss. The booklets were good and helpful and most of all they were a monthly reminder of the thoughtfulness of an acquaintance who really wanted to support me. I did not always stop and read them when they arrived but every time I saw one in the mail I was reminded of Jayne's thoughtfulness and care. That was the real blessing of the booklets.

My friend Terry, who I mentioned earlier, lost her husband when her children were young. At the time of Ned's death, she had been a widow for over 15 years. During the weeks and months after Ned died, Terry sent me amazing cards. The cards started coming about two weeks after the funeral and in them she shared her experience those many years ago when her young husband died. It was as if she were in my head and my house living my life. She talked about the thoughts I might be having and the things I was confronting and each of the cards was a reminder that this was a journey and I was not on the road alone. Terry was walking the path ahead of me and in these cards, she was sharing some of the milestones and obstacles she encountered. This was a real blessing in my life and a gift I will truly treasure forever.

Signpost:

For Others:

Take your clues from what the person dealing with the loss needs – not what you need to do or express. Listen and consider what the one who is grieving needs to move through the loss.

THE "DREADED" BOX

One of the experiences that is surprising, and in my experience never gets easier, is filling out paperwork that includes personal information after the death of a husband.

Checking the box "Married" just seemed the normal thing to do for 45 years. I was married and I was proud of the love and life we shared, and I wore beautiful diamond rings to broadcast that to everyone I met. It did not seem odd in most cases to check that box.

Now, one of the things I did not do was use the title "Mrs." most of the time. It always seemed to me that using that form of my name was more about him than me and as I said earlier no matter how much he was woven into the fabric of my life, and it was important to both of us to maintain independence. It was never a big deal. It is just the way we chose to introduce ourselves in public forums – Ned and Sharon Doty or Sharon and Ned.

When he died, it seemed as if I lost that option. There on every form I encounter is that dreaded box. I know now that those options were always there, but I never really saw them before. The choices are "single", "married", "widowed", and "divorced."

Now, just think about that for a moment. Who is "widowed"? A man is referred to as a "widower" if that moniker is used at all and in my more than 40 years serving on Boards and staffs of hospice organizations, I never heard a reference to a man being "widowed." A woman is "widowed" and, in fact, I know from talking with men who have lost their wives that only a woman is thrust into that cultural paradigm of "widowhood."

Now before you protest or think I am insensitive to the issues men confront when their spouse dies, I know that men who lose their wives to death have to deal with lots of new issues. I also know that some of the things I have experienced carry over to them.

However, the men I know who are dealing with the death of their wife quickly discover that the way society relates to me as a widow is a whole different world than the one they are experiencing. They are free to resume life and find new adventures for the most part. There are some who expect them to respond in a particular way – and mostly for all of us that is people who have never been through what we are dealing with. The difference is that they are not really confined to "widowhood" as a cultural phenomenon in our society the way that women experience it. Men still get invited to parties. They still play golf and go on fishing trips with their married friends. They still get invited to go places and have dinner with their couple friends. No one worries about their finances or how they are "handling" things.

The check mark "widowed" is a label that never goes away. It also provokes an entirely new relationship with the organization or entity that expects you to answer the question.

I have been told by some women - who have been alone for a long time due to their husband's extended illness or hospitalization when the husband is mentally no longer connected to reality - that being able after his death to mark the box "widowed" for the first time was somehow settling for them. They had for years been "married" - but not fully. At least now, checking the box for "widow" seemed accurate and settled the matter of their status.

For me and many others the question is why is the box for "widowed" even listed as a choice?

What is it intended to communicate that is a necessity or makes any real difference? What is checking that box meant to provide for the person filling out the form and what impact does that information have on the services or programs being offered?

After more than eight years, I am very clear what it provokes in me and in others and I continue to be baffled by the need for the question at all.

If a prospective landlord wants to know how many people will be living in the apartment and how they might be related, ask that question. If a doctor wants to know who is responsible for the bill – ask that question. If a banker has a special program for a certain population, just ask if the applicant qualifies. If there is a valid reason for knowing the marital status of anyone, just ask the question you need to have answered to provide the service. Whether I am married, single, widowed, or divorced does not answer any of these questions anyway. One is either married or single. Why one is "single" should not be important and smacks of an earlier time when a woman's value was determined by her marital status.

The fact is that as of March 23, 2011, I am not married. If there is a valid reason to ask about my marital status on a form, ask it. However, if there is no real justification for asking, why do so? No matter which box applies, checking the box puts the person in a category of people – it puts them in a "box."

When I have talked with others about this "box" the responses have been varied and interesting. Those that are married have no problem with the box for the most part. However, when I brought up the issue with others the response was quite different.

One friend who is divorced realized that every time she sees that box on a form, she has the same thoughts. What goes through her head is "They are going to see this and think I am a failure. They are probably going to think that my children are a mess and dealing with the aftermath of divorce." She said after talking with me about it she decided that from now on she is simply "single" if a box needs to be checked. No one needs to know that many years age she and her husband divorced. He is not responsible for anything where she is concerned.

Another friend shared with me that my conversation about the "dreaded box" reminded him that when his parents were killed in a car accident when he was seven, he now was an "orphan." He said that at age 67 he still thought of himself as an "orphan." He could see that this label had colored his picture of himself all his life.

So, the "dreaded box" provokes lots of different responses. What does that "widow" or "widowed" box provoke that is so challenging?

First, it prompts people to ask about the death of your husband and – once again - the ever-present comment "I am so sorry for your loss." Then there is a wall of sympathy that comes down and all sorts of assumptions from sudden concerns about whether you can take care of yourself when you don't feel well to worrying about whether you can get home safely after an event at night.

This last one is of particular interest to me as I continue to experience it over and over again. For years I have driven to Dallas from Tulsa to lead seminars and driven the same road home in the middle of the night – generally sometimes alone and sometimes with other women my age. No one ever gave that drive a second thought when my husband was alive – not even after he had a massive stroke and was virtually confined to the house.

However, now that I am a "widow", everyone is suddenly concerned that I drive by myself. How did that become a problem for them because he died? How did that become a concern because Ned is no longer alive? He slept through my trips home anyway. If he woke up during the night, he would often call to see where I was before he went back to sleep, but he was not worried about me driving home alone. Now people who don't really even know me well worry that I can't get home safely and all because I am a "widow." People now keep asking me to text them and let them know that I got home safely. I appreciate the concern for my well-being and am mystified that it only showed up after Ned died. Apparently, until then, even though he has suffered a serious stroke, they assumed he was doing the worrying.

I am glad people care but I wonder if they would expect the same thing if the one driving home alone late at night had been Ned. Something to think about…

The box is the beginning of that label being permanently attached to my life and my living and the world expects me to check the box for them presumably so they will know how to deal with me.

Why do I have to label myself a "widow"? Why am I expected to take on that mantel and wear it like sack cloth and ashes?

Every time I see the box, I am faced with an integrity issue I never saw coming. In reality, on that day in March of 2011, I was no longer married but for the world I am not "single", I am "widowed" and that means something *to* them, and it means something *for* me. Although I didn't understand that before Ned's death, it is something I confront frequently in this new world of widow that I am thrust into because he died before me.

Through this book I hope to be able to raise issues that allow us as a society to deal with some of these things in a way that is empathetic, caring, and respectful. In this case, it is easy. Just ask what you want to know and leave off the labels.

Whatever the label, whether it is single, married, widowed, or divorced, or whether you are an orphan or an only child or one among many siblings does not tell anyone anything about you. What difference does that label make in the care or customer service that is being provided? Look carefully to see how that label is coloring the way to see and interact with another person without ever getting to know the person as they are now.

This is certainly one time we could follow Elsa's advice from *Frozen* and "Let it go! Let it go!"

Signpost:

For Others:

Stop labeling people and putting them in boxes. No one is truly limited by the boundaries others place on the labels so let's just drop them altogether.

GRIEVING AND "MOURNING" TIME

We hear people say it all the time. "Grief is personal." The problem is that saying that is one thing and how we expect people to act is something entirely different – especially widows.

As I muddle through this new territory, I continuously encounter the remnants of a time in our society – not really so long ago – when women were considered property and if they were married, they could not own property in their own name, have their own bank account, or operate independent of their husbands.

Those who were not married were just considered "sad" and their marital status was "pitied". After all, what woman could really take care of herself? Men and many women were convinced that women were the "weaker" sex and needed a man to look after them to make it through this life.

It always puzzled me how that attitude could prevail if anyone actually looked at the lives of women and compared what they did to what the men they were married to actually took care of. For the most part, men earned the income. That may have taken hard work, so I am not discounting that, but the women cooked, cleaned, managed the household, birthed and raised the children and managed his day to day needs also. This weaker sex also survives him most of the time and, to me, that is no great surprise.

However, in this world I am discovering we are still dealing with a number of remnants of that time in our history when women's role and place was defined by the man she was attached to by marriage or family connection. Grieving and mourning fit in that category. Although most people would agree that grief is personal, they also have an opinion about how long a woman should be in "mourning" and how that should look.

There is an acceptable schedule and there are ways you are "supposed" to act during that time. There are also consequences if you don't conform. If you go back to work too soon, people question whether you are really dealing with the loss, whether you had to come back to work because he left you in financial trouble or whether you really cared that much about your husband after all. Sometimes they explain this away to each other (or to you) by asking questions about how much paid time off the company allowed or other inappropriate questions about your financial well-being.

At other times they talk to each other and speculate about why you would be coming back to work so soon and what that must mean about you, your relationship, and how you are dealing with the loss. They also often steer clear of you because they think they are supposed to give you room – or they just don't think they know the right thing to say. It is all about them – but they think it is about the widow.

You have to be careful not to have fun too soon either.

A laughing widow is a problem for a lot of people.

Never mind that the old adage "laughter is the best medicine" also applies to dealing with gut wrenching loss, it is just not appropriate for a widow to be laughing out loud too soon after her husband's death. Others will judge you for not reacting in the right way. I have even heard people use the word "unseemly" to describe a widow who is out in public enjoying life within weeks or even days of the funeral. Not so, by the way, with a widower.

Even without laughter there is the problem of not being sad enough or even drab enough. That old phrase about "sack cloth and ashes" is still very much a part of our culture for women experiencing the loss of a husband. It seems to be okay not to wear black all the time but don't be going overboard with bright colors and prints. That's just too much for others to deal with. You are not mourning in the proper way for the proper amount of time.

I cannot count the number of times I had to deal with judgmental comments from others about the fact that I was actively engaged in reinventing my life right after Ned died. For some reason, everyone I encountered expected me to explain myself – and inside this new cultural phenomenon "widow", I felt compelled to do just that.

Looking back, I can say both views are bizarre. What difference does it make what anyone does with their time and energy? Who are we to say that someone should be a particular way about dealing with a great loss? Why do I feel compelled to make you understand or make sure you feel better about what I am doing?

Grieving is personal! Mourning is personal, too, and there is no length of time that automatically attaches to that process. There is also no particular way it looks and no particular way it should go.

As I have said many times, Ned was woven into every fiber of the fabric of my life and yet we each were able to remain independent. His death ripped that fabric and no matter how great a job I do of rebuilding life without him, it will always be "life without him" since that day in 2011. How I do that is definitely up to me and it is sometimes difficult to communicate that to others around you or to stand up for yourself and say that you appreciate the concern, but it is really none of their business.

Most widows will just tolerate the questions rather than say something that might seem rude or hurt another's feelings. Widows are expected to deal with other people's questions, concerns, and considerations about us and how we are living our life with openness, generosity, and grace and to understand how they think we should be dealing with the loss.

A bit of advice for others - it is more than okay to be sad for her that life has been interrupted and refashioned in this way. Encourage her to rebuild and reinvent life in a new paradigm. Be grateful that she is moving forward. Be happy for her that she can reengage in life and begin to discover joy in the face of the change it is in life to lose a spouse. Trust her to know what she needs and unless she asks for your advice, keep it to yourself! Do not be the one that imposes your ideas, opinions, or points of view on her grieving and mourning. Do not let your judgments about how she is dealing with this loss stop you from reaching out in friendship or keep you from caring and supporting her.

Widows need to listen to their own needs and trust their own instincts. Sometimes it is valuable to hear other people's observations or views or to listen to their experiences of dealing with grief, but it is most important to remember that grief is personal. Focus on what you need, what you want, and what works for you.

Signpost:

For Others:

Honor the statement that "grief is personal" and let those around you who are dealing with loss grieve in the way that allows them to heal. Don't impose your own ideas of how it should go and don't judge them for not grieving the "right" way.

SLEEPING AND PLAYING ALONE

About six or seven years after Ned died, one Christmas Eve my then 10-year-old grandson came home with me after church to take care of my dog and get the presents at my house. I was spending the night at their house to be with them Christmas morning.

On the way to his house he said: "Grammy, you have to spend a lot of time alone now. Does it get boring?" I knew he was sincere in his question and I would not think of answering him with anything but the truth, so my answer was "Yes." We had a conversation about some of the things I am doing and actions I was taking to impact that.

He had clearly given this some thought because he had a suggestion of his own. He thought that the Tulsa branches of the family should create a schedule that included me in some way every day so that I would not be alone and bored. It made my heart smile to know that he was concerned for me and that he was thinking of ways to make it better particularly because I don't talk about being alone or bored – he just noticed and wondered.

This little one saw things that most people do not notice – not even me. This was the new "normal" for me. However, he sees me alone a lot of the time. He wonders about that and how I am coping with all that time by myself. For him, the changes in my life are not necessarily good for me. About a year earlier he told me that, in his opinion, I did not have enough human contact every day. Of course, at that time he also did not want to ride the bus home from school and was suggesting that I pick him up every day. He thought that in the five minutes it took to go from his school to his house, the human interaction I had with him would be good for me. Frankly, he was so original in his thinking that I agreed to drive the 30 minutes from my house to his school twice a week to do just that – take him to his home five minutes away. We all laughed about the ingenious way he got me to make the drive and pick him up but there was also some truth to what he was pointing to – and he was the only one noticing it and concerned about it.

For the most part I am fine being by myself. If I need help with something, I know how to ask for that help but I work hard to find a way to "do it myself." However, there is no way to really know what it will be like to sleep, pray, eat and play alone uninterrupted until you start to live life as a widow.

My family is great, and they too are busy with activities and lives that matter and make a difference. Most of the friends I have are married and they have no way of knowing what life is like for the widow among them. I am truly glad for that. I hope they never have to know that although odds are that they will.

It is hard to know when to speak up and when to just admit that things are different, and it is up to me to get used to the changes and find new ways to engage on my own. I have taken up crafting projects that I put down years ago. I have started new projects and found some new interests. And, as I said, I don't really have a problem being alone. It is just that there is a lot more alone time than I counted on.

Sleeping, eating, playing, and praying alone are just the beginning. There is also watching TV alone, cooking alone, shopping alone, doing chores that were once shared - alone. Decorating for Christmas alone and that includes buying a tree and getting it in the stand – alone. There is taking care of car maintenance – alone and carrying in the firewood – alone. It is all done alone now and that is a very different life for us than we ever had when he was alive.

If there is a widow in your life, from time to time ask her to join the festivities no matter how mundane they may be. If she is looking for some of that "human contact" my grandson was pointing to, she will take you up on the offer and join the festivities. If not, she will decline but I can tell you for sure she will appreciate that you asked. She will be moved that you noticed she is once again alone and offered to share some time with her.

Signpost:

For Others:

Take notice of those around you who live alone. Make room for them from time to time and let them know you noticed.

IT IS NOT THE SAME

Some say "A loss is a loss" but that's not really the case.

The nature of the relationship changes the nature and impact of the loss we experience. Although I have never experienced the loss of a child or a sibling, I have lost both of my parents, my grandparents – beginning with two of my Grandpas before I was seven, and my husband of 45 years. The losses, each painful and devastating in their own way, are not the same.

I always knew that I had no way of knowing what a parent goes through with the loss of a child. It seems that would be the most painful, inconsolable kind of loss imaginable. One of my dearest friends lost her son to suicide, and I knew just watching her and being with her that some part of her died with him – even though she dealt really powerfully with the entire thing. The love she had for her other children and her husband sustained them both during the years after his death but that pain of losing one she gave birth to never really subsided. That does not mean that she did not smile or laugh or have a great life after his death. It is just that there was a damper on everything except the work she did in support of mental health issues for young people who were struggling and the care she provided others as a hospice volunteer.

When my mother died, there was a hole in my heart that was hard to explain or deal with and yet, I still have such a connection with her that I have the experience that she comes to check up on me from time to time and lets me know she is there supporting and loving me from a different place. That loss too was unique. My friend Leslie asked me shortly after Mom's death what it was like to lose your mother. My answer was that it is weird. It's weird not being on the same planet as the person who gave birth to you. I can't imagine not experiencing some kind of disconnect when that happens no matter what your relationship is with your mother. She still gave you life and when that life source dies, something is different in your life. Still, it is the natural order of things that mothers die before daughters and no matter how painful, it is not unexpected or unimaginable.

The death of my husband was quite something different from all of the losses I had suffered before. This man was not my flesh and blood. We were not descended from each other in the way that parents, children and siblings are connected. He was woven into the fabric of my life by choice – mine and his. He did not give me life, but he was an integral part of life for me and together we created life in our three children.

Losing him was not the same as losing my mother or grandparents. It was not the same a losing my dearest friends (which has happened twice in my life so far) and not the same as the loss of close family members.

Losing him literally tore the fabric of my life in two. For more than 50 years he was part of the creation of that fabric. The threads of his life were woven through mine and the threads of my life were woven through his.

They were intertwined and came together to create a multitude of magnificent patterns that were made up of the experiences, activities, loving and living of two lives given to and for each other over many years. Interrupting that weaving because of the death of one of the parties involved tears apart the very fabric of that life. The memories remain but the experiences, activities, loving, and living are finished forever.

One thing I will never do again is assume that I know what someone is experiencing as a result of the loss of a loved one. I know what the experience has been like for me in each case and I know what it feels like when someone who lost a parent or a sibling assumes that they know what I am experiencing in the loss of my husband – because they have experienced loss. I have discovered for myself that when that happens, I am left with the experience that my loss has been diminished or minimized in some way and I never want to leave anyone else with that experience.

These days if someone loses a parent or spouse or child, I simply express my sympathy and offer to listen to whatever they need to say about the person or the loss. I don't try to pretend I know what they are going through. I just let them know that I am interested in hearing anything they have to say about what's happening for them – without judgment and without expectations. Letting them know that whatever they are experiencing is unique to them and is fine is, in my humble opinion, the best way that I can honor and respect their loss and, at the same time, give them the freedom and space to express whatever they need to say without minimizing or diminishing what they are dealing with.

Signpost:

For Widows and For Others Experiencing Loss:

Remember that each loss is unique, and each person's experience of loss is personal. Be careful not to minimize their experience or yours by comparing their loss to yours.

EXPERIENCING GRIEF BOMBS

When you lose a spouse, there is an acute feeling of loss that is indescribable even if the loss is not totally unexpected.

For many years Ned and I lived as though he would die at age 56. After all, his father and five generations of men before him had all died at age 56 of a condition that Ned was diagnosed with in his mid-twenties. We lived our lives as if we had a specific time period to experience living and loving each other and we lived it without regret or resentment. It was just the way it was.

In that picture of the future, from time to time I often tried to imagine what life would be like for me after he was gone. In fact, I was sure I knew how things would go. The truth is that this is nothing like what I thought it would be - nothing at all.

Ned lived to be 68 so we had many more years than first expected and I am grateful for every day we got after his 57th birthday. But even the expectation that I would be left behind did not prepare me for the profound grief I experienced every day after his death. The grief manifested itself in many different ways and it was not always an experience of tears and feeling bad. Sometimes it was just the feeling of loss and being alone in a big empty house. Sometimes it was the absence of noise and sometimes just a moment when I wanted to share something funny with him and he was not there to listen or ask him a question about something he always handled.

A couple of months after he died I was driving home from a graduation dinner celebrating my niece Ashley and started to call him and tell him I was headed to the house. As I picked up the phone in the car, I realized there was no one to call. Sometimes these moments were like a "gut punch" and other times they were moments of profound sadness.

Over the months after his death the acute and consistent feeling of loss and grief began to wane. I was on the pathway to discovering a new normal for my life and no matter how much I missed him, moving forward did not involve thinking of him in almost every moment.

However, to this day there is the phenomenon my friend Leslie called "grief bombs". They are unexpected moments of loss and pain and they seem to come from out of nowhere and explode in the middle of my life. They can be triggered by almost anything and are often sparked by the most unexpected things. Most of the time they seem to be so random that I have no idea what triggered them. That does not lessen the pain or soften the blow or slow the onslaught of tears.

When I shared about "grief bombs" with my children they knew exactly what I was talking about. Moments when someone or something just triggers a memory and the missing of that loved one is present, and as real as it was at the time of the loss.

It goes away almost as quickly as it came, and life goes on as before. I have come to expect the "grief bombs" as momentary expressions of a mixture of joy and pain

- joy at the memory of times passed that are treasured and valued beyond measure, and pain at the resurgence of the tearing at the heart that comes with the re-experiencing the loss. I never want to lose either.

My husband died in 2011 and I realize that many think I should be past it now and moving on – and in most ways I am. I do not dwell in the loss but I also do not turn away from the moments that remind me of the joy of loving him, the gift of family we created, the memories shared through a lifetime and the missing it is for me that he is no longer here to hug and talk to and snuggle with under the covers on a winter night.

Grief bombs are my reminder of all that was shared as well as the loss of that life. They are a fact of life and one I expect to experience for the rest of my life.

Signpost:

For the Widow and For Others Experiencing Loss:

Be prepared for grief bombs and just let them be a reminder of love and loss.

BECOMING INVISIBLE

Lunch with a friend of mine who has experienced widowhood twice in her life shined a light on something else that I had simply become accustomed to since he died. Although she is not someone who dwells in the negative, she also does not sugar coat anything and has no problem being really straight about what's happened or what she is dealing with. In response to something I said about only being seen as a widow, she said, "They probably don't even see you at all. When my husband died, I became invisible to a lot of people."

That is part of the journey that I have not paid much attention to. I am pretty good at making my presence known when I need to, but when I looked at my life since my husband's death, I realized she was right.

For a lot of people, I am invisible.

When I talk with other women who are divorced or single by choice, they admit they have a similar experience. The world is designed for couples and not being part of one often leaves you with the experience of being invisible.

One example that happens more than you can imagine is that restaurant seating staff look past me to the people behind me because they either don't see me standing there or they are sure I must be waiting for someone or, perhaps because I am a woman alone, they think I belong with the group behind me. There are any number of times and places where a woman alone is invisible. Sometimes, if they are busy, restaurant seating staff don't want to give one person a whole table so they pretend they don't see you or that others came in ahead of you.

Have you ever walked through the door of some place with a group of people you don't know and had the people inside assume you were with them? That happens all the time to widows.

Have you ever picked the wrong place for a vacation and found out that there does not seem to be anyone in the entire place that is not part of a couple? I have and I have learned not to vacation alone at wedding and honeymoon destinations.

Have you ever had someone taking tickets or seating people at an event look past you to take the people behind you? I have and so have a great many other widows (and, I am guessing, other single women).

When I walk in a restaurant the seating staff assumes I am waiting for someone. I get that but it does not change that saying that over and over in response to "How many tonight?" is a constant reminder that I am now alone most of the time. To deal with this I have started beating them to the punch. When the person seating customers looks at me, I say "Table for one please." This leave me in control and eliminates that inevitable look of "Oh, poor you" that some just can't hide. I also know women who are single for whatever reason deal with the same thing.

Living as a widow is not an option for me. It is my new way of life - and I am okay with that. It is just what's so. I have no desire to change that "widow" status to "married" again so it would be great if the world stopped relating to me and other single women as if we are alone by accident or default or that we are victims of some temporary tragedy we are desperately trying to remedy.

I am not invisible, and neither is that woman over there by herself or the one shopping alone at the grocery store or the one who just came in the theatre by herself. We are women who live, work, and play in life and we happen to be single. Notice us but don't feel sorry for us. Most of us have options – we just say "No! We are just fine."

Signpost:

For Others:

Take time to notice everyone. No one is invisible – even those who are alone. Remember that some are alone by circumstance and some are alone by choice – and neither is invisible or in need of pity.

HE IS STILL WITH YOU!

Some "widowomen" and I have talked recently about this cultural conversation about our husbands still being with us.

There is no doubt for any of us that the spiritual or soulful connection to our husbands is still there. Heck, we still talk to him a lot. What we are clear about is that this continuing connection we are experiencing is not the same as what others seem to be talking about when they say things like "He is still by your side."

Actually, no, he is not still here. He is gone. He did not "transition" or "pass" or "go on ahead." He died and he is not coming back. I am never going to feel his arms around me again in this life. He is not going to carry on a conversation with me or help with the driving to Kansas or Georgia to see the grandkids. He is not going to mow the lawn or change the lightbulbs or make jokes that make me laugh so hard I cry. He is not going to balance the checkbook, or go with me to the theater, or kneel beside me in prayer at church. He is not here!

I wonder sometimes if the comments are more about wishful thinking because they are almost always made by someone whose spouse is still living. Maybe it is easier to deal with my loss and the prospect of theirs someday by making it not so bad – not so final – not so certain.

I don't know what is there for them. What I do know is that my love for him is still with me. My memories of the best of times and the worst of times are still stored in my brain and are available any time day or night that I call on them. The pictures on the wall bring smiles of recollection and warm feelings of love and care. The poster with his favorite sayings reminds me of his wit and wisdom. These things I have and will always have. However, he is not here!

The reality of this was never as present for me as it was a few years ago when I was named one of the "50 Making a Difference in Oklahoma" and honored as a candidate for "Woman of the Year" for Oklahoma.

As I was preparing to go to Oklahoma City for the event, I was excited, humbled, and sad because the three people that recognition would mean the most to – my mother, my father, and my husband – would not be there to sit beside me and see what they had nurtured into being.

Everyone I mentioned this to had the same response. "They will be there with you." I believe that they were with me in spirit but just so you know, it is not the same.

In the end, I was there surrounded by my children, one of my grandchildren, and two of my brothers and I was still very much there without the three people whose love and support made it possible. I believe they know – and they were not there!

It is okay to let us miss them. No one has to remind us of the connection we had that will never go away.

Sometimes it seems like these comments about him still being there diminish the loss and disrespect the grief. I know that's not the purpose but that's often how it feels. Just let us be with the missing him. It is okay! We do and that's just what's so. You don't have to find a way to soften that or make me feel better. I am fine – and I miss my husband and saying that does not mean anything more than just that. I am fine and I miss my husband. Thanks for caring. I appreciate it very much.

Signpost:

For Others:

You don't have to soften the blow of the loss or find a way to make it better. It's okay. We know the person is gone for good. Just let us be with the loss in whatever way works for us.

EATING ALONE – THERE IS A DIFFERENCE

On a segment of one of the network morning news shows the anchors commented on posts by a celebrity that she had enjoyed going out to eat alone. Everyone at the table agreed that there were times when eating alone is a real treat. No kids demanding attention. No friends that want you to listen to their problems. No noise!

But there is a difference. Choosing to eat alone as a unique experience that is a "treat" is a lot different from eating alone every day because you there is no longer someone there to share a meal with.

Most days I eat alone at home by choice. In the years since Ned's death, cooking for myself and eating alone has become the routine. However, that was not the case right after he died. I ate at home alone then too but there were many times when I would just go out to a restaurant to be in an environment of noise and energy. Even if I was at a table alone, the sounds of the restaurant and the people sharing meals together was comforting in an odd way. Without anyone left at home to talk to or listen to; without anyone in the house that made noise or generated activity, the silence was sometimes oppressive.

There is a good deal of research that eating alone is not healthy. The scientists say that we are more likely to eat more and to eat unhealthy foods when we are alone and that can have a detrimental effect on us.

Recent research studies on several health issues have found that social activities, eating meals with others, and being engaged in a community all have positive impacts on health and wellbeing as well as longevity.

In my experience much of this is true but how you deal with the situation is personal. For example, I have come a long way from the need to go out to noisy restaurants to eat in order to fill my life with sound after Ned's death. Sometimes that is what I want and need – like when I just need to get in the car and head out to some place with lots of people and energy. However, when I go out to eat alone now, it is more likely because what I want to eat cannot be found in my pantry or I just want to be waited on and not have to clean up the mess.

Eating alone is not necessarily my choice but it is my life. I have become very good at cooking for one or cooking things that can be frozen for later. I will admit that I am not as creative or inventive when cooking as when he was alive or before the kids left home, but I like eating in the comfort of my own home and I like knowing what is in the food I am cooking. Food has become less about socialization and more about nourishment. That's a good thing!

My advice to widows is to trust what you need and do what works in this area too. If you need to find friends that eat with you – do that! If you need to go enjoy a meal in a noisy restaurant – do that! If you want to eat at home alone, whether it is take-out or home cooked – do that!

There are no rules here. The fact is that you are now alone. Eating is just one of the things you will now be doing by yourself that you were usually doing with him. The best advice I can give is to do what works for you and ask for what you need and at the end of the day, take care of yourself. That means – eat healthy, eat moderately, and eat well. You are all you have right now, and you are counting on you to take good care!

Signpost:

For the Widow and For Others Experiencing Loss:

Eating alone is not necessarily a bad thing. It really is up to the individual.

SURPRISING AND UNPREDICTABLE MOMENTS

One Saturday night as I was headed home from singing at church, I realized there was nothing to eat at my house. So, I stopped at an Italian restaurant in the neighborhood and went in to wait my turn. The greeter told me that the wait was at least 20 minutes, so I found a place to sit and made myself comfortable. There was another family in the alcove where I was sitting, and they smiled and said "Hello". The young boy with them announced to me that they were there to celebrate his eighth birthday.

A few minutes later the mom asked me if I was there alone. When I said that I was, she asked if I wanted to join them for dinner. I was surprised and delighted to be included. So, we became one table of 6 for dinner instead of two tables, one for 5 and another for 1.

Not only did they invite me to join them, but they refused to let me buy my own dinner and even when I offered to buy appetizers they said "No." A friend who worked at the restaurant had already taken care of that. During dinner I discovered that the Dad had a floor refinishing business and worked with local contractors; that mom worked with Dad and at a local restaurant; and that their two daughters were finishing high school nearby and that one had ambitions to be an orthodontist and the other aspired to be a pediatrician.

I also found out that their grandmother lived in Mexico and was not there to celebrate the birthday. The birthday boy was glad to have a "grandma" with him that night. It seems that since coming to the United States nine years earlier they had not seen their grandmother. As the young boy was born in this country and the girls were very young when they came to America, they didn't know what it was like to have a grandmother and so I got to contribute that to the evening.

As we shared all kinds of things, I learned why mom invited me to join them. She was terribly afraid of being alone. She saw me alone and was worried about me. It was mystifying to her that I could be okay with being alone and that I could live alone all the time. That seemed to her like the scariest thing ever. Later, when I realized that this is the family that the conversations about illegal immigrants and "dreamers" are about, I could understand better the fear she has and why it paralyzes her. In her culture family and being included is everything. She truly thought it was that way for everyone.

As we were preparing to leave, the dad says to me "Not all of us are bad people." At first, I was confused and then I realized that he was talking about their immigration status. I immediately assured him that the thought never crossed my mind.

Driving home, I was thinking about the miracle the evening was. First, in the years since Ned's death that is only the second time that someone has invited me to join them for a meal while we were waiting for a table – and the first time was during a snowstorm in Joplin when the restaurant was really busy. That person turned out to be someone responsible for child sexual abuse prevention education in that part of the state and I was later retained as their Keynote speaker at the spring conference.

This time I got to know a family that I might never have encountered. Mom and Dad who came to this country to find a better life and left behind a family they love and miss. Add to that two "dreamers" who were brought here at the ages of six and eight by their parents and a young son, not eight years old who was born here and is a natural born citizen. They work hard. They support themselves. They pay taxes and care for their community. They want a future and they live in fear.

Thank you to the family for inviting me to share their evening, their table, and a few moments of their life. Thank you to these wonderful, caring people who could not stop themselves from reaching out to the older woman waiting to have dinner alone in a crowded noisy restaurant and inviting her to be part of their celebration.

That night I was not invisible, and neither were they. It was surprising, unpredictable and delightful. We should all have more of those experiences in life. Just thinking about it brings a smile to my face every time.

Signpost:

For the Widow and For Others Experiencing Loss:

Take time to enjoy and appreciate the unpredictable and surprising opportunities that crop up from time to

time. Be grateful for the unexpected gifts that others bring to your life.

UNSOLICITED OPINIONS AND INTRUSIVE QUESTIONS

If my brothers read this, they will be able to fill in the blank in this statement without even thinking: "Opinions are like a**holes, everybody's got one." It was one of my Dad's favorite sayings to remind us that opinions are a dime a dozen.

Most of the time other people's opinions are worth listening to, but that does not mean that you have to adopt them as your own. In my experience as a widow, those opinions sometimes show up in the form of strange or even inappropriate questions.

One cultural phenomenon I discovered is that there is a whole world of opinion out there about how I should be, how I should act, what I should need, and how I should now live my life – all because I am a widow. Almost none of what the world thinks should be is accurate for me but that does not stop people thinking or expressing these points of view. It also does not keep them from expecting me to act and live my life the way I "should" or from agreeing with them that their opinion is the best one for all concerned - meaning me.

It is not hard to see that there is no shortage of opinions in the world. It is also clear that everyone thinks theirs is the right one and the one that others should adopt as their own. However, there is one aspect of this world of widowhood and the swirl of opinion that surrounds us that is a bit different. In this world, opinions take on a life of their own and there are lots of expectations of how I should respond to them.

Before Ned died, if someone had an opinion about what I was doing or how I was being they usually kept it to themselves – unless I asked. If they shared it with me, it was offered as an "opinion" and included reasons and justifications for the ideas put forth. For example, if they thought I was missing something in my business that could make a difference, they would tell me what they saw as missing but leave it to me and my good judgment to deal with the issue. If they did not like the way I was doing something, they would sometimes make a suggestion and at other times just did it themselves.

Taking the lessons from my dad to heart, there are three practices I have adopted over the years around opinions and intrusive questions that have had a profound impact on the amount of drama and upset in my life.

First, I work hard to give others the respect I expect which means keeping my opinions to myself unless I am asked.

Second, I avoid asking people about their personal, private business unless there is some urgent, appropriate reason.

Finally, several years ago I took on the practice of not listening to complaints about anyone or anything that I could not directly do something about. It is hard to imagine the difference these three practices have made in my life. Life is simpler, more enjoyable, and a lot less dramatic.

However, I am discovering that as a widow I am not always afforded the same courtesy with regard to the first two practices – other peoples' opinions and intrusive questions about my private or personal business. People seem to think they know what I am dealing with – and how I should deal with it – and that they have the right to share that with me at any time and in any situation. In fact, they often act as if I have been waiting to hear from them to get the matter resolved. They also think they are entitled to ask me intrusive questions about my personal life and private business – and it should be okay with me.

One day I was in a business conference and one of the leaders that I knew and had worked with for many years turned to me and said, "Did Ned leave you financially okay or do you still have to work?" I was stunned into silence and as I sat there looking at the concerned expression on his face, I realized he really thought I should tell him whether I was financially okay – for some reason.

I looked at him and said "Before I respond, let me ask you a question. If the person sitting here were Ned rather than me, would you be asking that question?" He shocked himself when he answered "No!"

The only reason he asked me that question was a "concern" of his - some idea in the back of his mind - that husbands should leave their wives financially settled. The other interesting aspect of this conversation is that this was someone I had worked with for years and had never heard make a sexist comment or assume skills or limitations based on gender and yet – here he was asking this completely inappropriate, intrusive question.

This question has been asked to others, too. In fact, in one instance, a widow's brother was contacted by a mutual friend after the brother-in-law died suddenly. This mutual friend wanted to find out the same thing – whether my friend's sister would be okay financially after the death. None of the people making these inquiries had any financial responsibility for the widow and none were intending to offer assistance. They just thought it was okay to ask because she was a widow and surely she would understand they were just making sure she would be financially taken care of by her husband.

The funny thing is that the people with these opinions and questions are not widows or even widowers. They are also not members of my family, close friends, or people I am asking for help. They are convinced, however, that they have the answers for me about all sorts of things if I would just answer their questions or heed and adopt their unsolicited opinions.

Other people's opinions are just that – other people's opinions. They are entitled to their opinion as I am to mine. From this perspective I can view the continuous unsolicited advice and opinions about how I should live my life since Ned's death as a by-product of widowhood.

What is unusual is that this is what society apparently thinks I need and because I am now a widow, I'm expected to accept these gracious comments in the spirit in which they were intended - whether I want it or need it or not. It is one more way that society's view of widows is distinct.

Now, I am not saying that some of the opinions might not be useful. It's just that they are offered as "the answer" not as an opinion or suggestion. Never do I hear "In my opinion..." or "You might consider..." or "If you are interested..." as opening phrase. Usually the sentence starts with some versions of "You should..."

From time to time it is clear that the opinion being offered is from a genuine concern or even because you have expressed frustration or concern about something. In those cases, it might seem that the opinions are less about widowhood and more about friendship or compassion. However, it really depends on who is doing the talking, what they are talking about, and who they are talking to.

In addition to being the recipient of unsolicited opinions from all sorts of people, for almost all the widows that I have met, there is another common experience. Family members, friends, and even acquaintances think it is fine to discuss our "situation" with each other and come up with plans for us that they think are the best way to deal with what we are dealing with.

For example, I found out that my children were talking with each other about what I should do about any number of things, including where I should move. They were all genuinely concerned for me and worried that I might be making decisions too quickly and not giving enough thought to the long-term consequences.

The problem was not that they were concerned – I could appreciate that.

The problem was that they were not talking to me about any of this.

I have a great relationship with my children, and we have an agreement in this family that we don't keep secrets – even if they might be hard to talk about or painful. So, I called my youngest to ask her if she and her sister were talking about me and not including me in the conversation. She said that, in fact, they had talked but more to process their own opinions and consider what to do or say to make sure I understood their concerns and took enough time to make major decisions.

My kids are amazing, and I could see there was nothing but love and concern being expressed. So, all I did was request that they include me in the conversation. I promised to listen to their concerns and when they heard my response and what I was thinking about, they realized that I was taking time and giving serious consideration to matters I was dealing with before making a decision.

They were my children and they were worried about me. I understood how they might be concerned and was able to share with them that part of my reaction to finding out they were talking to each other about me was that this kind of thing was happening with other people too. People in my life who never had any concern about my ability to take care of myself before were suddenly worried about me and the only reason was that I was now a "widow."

One of the things we all saw out of this experience was the pull of that societal conversation that widows are somehow helpless and needy. Even my children – who knew better – realized that they were caught in the societal concern that I would somehow lose myself or my way because of their father's death.

After our conversation, my daughter Shannon started to notice how this attitude is reinforced in many ways in society. For example, she pointed out that the commercials for life saving alert systems always show an older woman who has fallen and can't get up. A woman alone is always the one in trouble.

Another friend of mine found out that her friends had decided she should be going out and having fun and perhaps even dating just a few months after her husband's death. They set her up and told her to go. She felt compelled to go because she could see they had good intentions and she did not want to hurt their feelings. The problem was they were doing it because they thought it would be good for her – not because it was what she wanted. She was not even part of the plan. Their opinion was dictating the action and they had not even shared it with her.

One thing experience this has taught me is the value of those three practices I mentioned earlier. Life is much less complicated when I do.

I am also reminded that there is value in sharing an experience rather than an opinion. For example, if I have encountered a similar issue, I might share with the person how I dealt with it and how my action or inaction worked or did not work. The point is that I am committed that this book let widows – and others who are suffering significant loss – know that they are the only ones who know how they should be doing their life. There is no way they "should" be being or acting, no opinion they have to adopt, and no intrusive, private question they need to answer for anyone unless they choose to do so.

It is impossible to stop having opinions. It is also normal to be curious about things you have concerns about. However, it is entirely possible to stop yourself from acting on that curiosity or spouting your opinions as if you have the answer for other people.

Signpost:

For Others:

More listening, more sharing, and less opining will create a more loving, caring, supportive, and compassionate environment for everyone.

AND NOW COME THE HOLIDAYS

Wow! No matter how "prepared" one is for the holiday season after the death of a husband, it is not ever easy.

I love Christmas. I love the decorations, the music, the dorky sweaters, the holiday spirit, and all the other aspects of the season. Ned loved it, too, and he had a new experience after the movie "The Santa Clause". You see, he looked almost exactly like Tim Allen in that movie (after Tim gained the weight and his hair and beard turned white). Ned even wore those ridiculous Christmas sweaters and had a big beard during the winter.

He looked so much like the Santa in that movie that when we went to see it in the theater and the lights came up at the end of the movie, the children sitting around us gasped when he stood up. He played along and winked and smiled at all of them. I heard them saying "It's him! It's him!" to their parents as the movie theater owner came up and asked if he could just hang around the theater during this run. The following Sunday at Mass he was preaching and as he walked to the Lectern, a small child's voice could be heard from the back rows saying, "See Mom, I told you Santa Claus went to our Church."

Ned loved this season and loved being Santa Claus for children and adults. He loved decorating. He loved shopping on his own and buying weird gifts for everyone – including a jigsaw puzzle for every member of the family every year, whether people wanted them or not. He loved creating light displays outside and putting up a huge, real tree in the living room in front of a window.

For us the week between Christmas and New Year's was a very special time. We made sure that we had that time together to be with each other. We took day trips together. We read books and cooked fun things and watched movies and played games. It was a very special time for us as a couple.

Then he died, and I had no idea what to do with myself. Decorating did not have the same interest for me that first year. My beautiful collection of Father Christmas dolls were left in their boxes in the attic and for the first time in my life I did not put up a Christmas tree. I still loved the music and the singing, but it really was not the same and I had no idea how to reinvent the holidays without Ned. Somehow, I was totally unprepared for how difficult this would be without him.

The week after Christmas became a dreaded time. It is truly the hardest week of the year for me to be a "widow" because it was a most special time for us as a couple. The first year I was truly depressed. Having lived with someone who was constantly dealing with clinical depression I knew the signs and I had them all. I could not get out of bed unless there was somewhere I had to be or someone was expecting me. I sat on the sofa and watched old movies and reruns of TV shows. I did not eat. I did not call anyone, and I desperately wanted to drink – but I had no alcohol and getting some meant getting dressed and leaving the house, so I did without.

On New Year's Day that first Christmas, I went to Mass to begin the New Year and prayed for a way out of the mire I felt stuck in, and a few days later I started to see the sunlight again and get out in life. One thing I learned during that time was to prepare for it in years to come. I am vulnerable at Christmas time to melancholy and depression. If I want to have joy and peace and love during that time, I have to make it happen. Now I plan things for that week before New Year's. I either leave my house to go somewhere else or I plan projects and activities with others so that I am not alone at home any day that week.

Christmas was not the only holiday I had to deal with and when I realized that it was critical that I find new ways to celebrate, I started to create new practices and ways to celebrate.

At Thanksgiving on the odd numbered years when my children were with their spouses' families, I volunteered at community meals for those in need. I worked until lunch was over and the kitchen was cleaned up and then took a plate of turkey and dressing home to eat as I watched football.

At Christmas I took on a new practice of choosing someone(s) off the Angel Tree and spending on them what I would have spent on Ned. So, the person I chose usually gets everything on his or her list. I also chose an older child or young adult as everyone wants the kids. If the person only asks for something small, I take two or three names. Saint Paul reminds us in

Galatians that living a life in the spirit means having your attention and eyes on the needs of others. This has proven to be very nurturing for me during this time of year.

Christmas trees are special to me and I looked for a new way to bring life to that tradition. One way that has been accomplished is that I also started having the grandkids come over to decorate my tree – and every year it is unique and special. I put out the Father Christmas dolls and put up an artificial tree because now I am gone over the holidays.

We loved being home for Halloween and meeting all the goblins, ghosts, and princesses, and pirates that rang our doorbell. After Ned's death Halloween became a time I went to the home of my youngest and took on handing out candy to the children who came by while their family participated in the neighborhood parade and went "trick or treating" with their children.

Easter is hard work for Catholics in ministry. Ned was an ordained Deacon and for most of my life I have served as a Church Music Director. We usually went to the buffet at the Doubletree Downtown in Tulsa and then went home to take a nap. Ned spent the afternoon watching a golf tournament on TV. Now, if I am home, I sing at all the celebrations and then either take a nap and watch movies or do something fun. One year I drove 90 miles on Easter Sunday to watch the OU Women's Basketball team play Tennessee in the Sweet 16 of the NCAA Tournament. Easter Sunday dinner was a dripped beef sandwich at the arena – new practices and new experiences.

For Valentine's Day I sometimes prepare and send special cards to my grandchildren or to someone who normally gets left out of that celebration.

For Ned's birthday, I do something that honors him. This year I hosted a dinner for our faith sharing group that night and before everyone left, I told them it was his birthday and we said a special prayer of Thanksgiving for the gift of his life and faith in our lives.

My Wedding Anniversary has become the most special holiday of all. The children are a bit spread out now across the country, but for the first few years we gathered together on that day – just the four of us – at a nice restaurant to celebrate the day Ned and I made a new family. We are that family on earth now and no matter where we are, when the date of the anniversary rolls around there are special thoughts, wishes, and expressions of love shared between the four of us.

Holidays will never be the same again but that does not mean they cannot be good or that there is nothing to celebrate or enjoy. What it does mean is that I will miss him more on those days than at any other time of the year and those moments will be occasions to remember many joy-filled moments from 45 years of living and loving before he was gone from this world.

Do what works for you. Celebrate or don't. Skip it or create new traditions. Recreate holidays past or reinvent new celebrations.

The most important thing is to be honest about what you need. It is not your job to do anything for anyone else or to make them happy or to have them feel okay. Do what you need to do take care of you.

Signpost:

For Others:

Be respectful of the needs of people experiencing significant loss to create new experiences and new traditions around holidays. Let them know you support them in whatever way they need.

STILL FEELING MARRIED

There is one piece of this process that seems to apply equally to widows, widowers, and divorced individuals.

Being single again is a challenge to everyone today.

Whether you were married for five minutes or 75 years, when your spouse/partner is gone, you are suddenly seeing life through different eyes.

One problem is that you still feel married. You still see life through that filter. Those who were together for a number of years and have children together don't really know any other way to be or live and yet there you are – single again – and in a whole new world.

In my experience, living single again can only be described as a minefield. After being an intimate part of another person's life for over 50 years, being single was definitely foreign territory and I had no idea how to navigate it.

In today's world being single is not only unfamiliar as an experience of being in life, but it is unlike anything in our memory of what it was to be single. Single life today is like entering a parallel universe.

Although this phenomenon of discovering "being single again" is a common to everyone who loses a spouse or partner, there is an added element when the person is a "widowoman."

We used to have a saying in the hospice care world - "Women remember - men remarry." Society seems to find comfort in a widower finding someone new to share his life with and those who are divorced are encouraged by their friends and family to "get back out there." In my experience society's view of what a widow should do is quite different. There is no universal view of the subject but there are about four different points of view that seem to prevail.

First, there are the people that expect you to live alone and spend the rest of your life paying tribute to the life you lived with your husband. If living alone is your choice, that's great. However, choosing to live as a single person is different from living alone to pay tribute to the life you had with your husband. The people in this group keep having conversations with you about your life with your husband. The way this group sees widows reminds me of old movies that include older widowomen who are dumpy, wear black all the time, and cook for everyone. That's fine for those that choose it but – not for me.

There is another group that thinks that "after an appropriate length of time" you should meet some new people and start dating again and explore that possibility. I can't tell you how many people gave me unsolicited advice about dating apps and how to meet men as a widowoman. In fact, some of them thought I should get out there and find a new man right away. One person challenged me to get on a dating app about six months after Ned died. This idea I should rush to find the next man was startling to me. It felt as though the people pushing me toward dating were concerned that I might not be able to make it on my own or even that I needed a man in my life to be whole and complete.

A third group lets you know pretty quickly that they will be judging and assessing any man that shows an interest in you. Some friends and acquaintances made it clear to me that they would be evaluating any man to determine whether he was worth of me – and they would let me know.

In those moments it felt as though I were 16 again and my parents were demanding to meet some young man who asked me out so they could decide if he was okay for me to see. I could tell that the people in this group were well-meaning and only interested in assuring that any man I dated was worth it – but it did seem a bit odd to encounter that point of view from so many people in my life.

The fourth group is family. For children and grandchildren, the introduction of a new man into the picture is frightening and unsettling. There are unrealistic and largely unfounded fears that their parent or grandparent will be lost and forgotten if you find a new man to share any part of your life with. And, of course, children think their parents are asexual, so there is the fact that they have to deal with you having feelings and emotions just like any other red-blooded adult.

If you are aware of this societal attitude, you can have some fun with it and still live life on your terms. For example, the Thanksgiving after Ned died I decided I wanted to go somewhere different and do something he and I had never done. So, I went to Missouri and enjoyed Thanksgiving dinner with my son-in-law's family. There were about 30 people there including Chris's uncle David, who was a builder and a friend of Ned's. There were also neighbors and other family members in the group. David and I had a lot to talk about and catch up on and we sat next to each other at the table. On the way home my daughter told me that while she and the neighbor were clearing the table the woman asked her how long David and I had been dating. We all got a good laugh out of that and the kids pointed out that I should be feeling good that the neighbor thought I was with David since he was at least 15 years younger than me. The grandkids labeled me a "cougar."

Being single at age 68 was a revelation to me. One of the things that puzzled me was how interested everyone else was in the subject of my being single and possibly dating and how they assumed that I would just automatically join in the current world of dating. One friend asked me one day how I planned to explain it to my children when they showed up at my house some morning and encountered a man having breakfast with me. My response was that there would not be any men spending the night with me so that was not a problem. This Irish Catholic girl could not even imagine going down that road.

The important thing to remember is that you have to do what works for you. In the years since Ned's death I have considered dating. I tried a dating site for seniors and met a couple of nice men that I enjoyed talking to – once or twice. I even met with a professional matchmaker. During that interview is when I realized that I have no interest in that pathway and three years later I am good with that decision.

No matter what age you are as a widow, new adventures are available. Whether that adventure means traveling that road as a single person or finding new love it is important to do what works for you.

Let others know that you appreciate their concern (if you do) and remind them that you are an adult and can make your own decisions. Live the life you want – the one that enriches your new life experience.

Signpost:

For the Widow:

Don't let others decide what's the right path for your future. You get to say whether the road you take is the familiar and comfortable one or the one less traveled that is filled with the unknown. There is no wrong road if you choose it for yourself.

TRAVELING ALONE

A few months ago, I returned from the trip of a lifetime to the British Isles and, in particular, Ireland. It was magical and wonderful and although I was on a tour bus with 23 other people and a dear friend traveled with me, I was really traveling alone. It is hard for those who have never been married and those who still are – even if they are by themselves on the trip – to really get "traveling alone."

There were two widows on the trip – me and one other woman. The other widow did not seem to have anything good to say about her husband. In the beginning of the trip it seemed she did not really like him very much. By the time the trip was winding down she had mellowed a bit and shared a few stories with us about good times with him, but I was really left with the sense that she was happy to be by herself.

The places we went and the things we saw were different than any I ever experienced with Ned. He and I took one amazing trip to Italy and Switzerland but that was it. He never made it to Ireland or Alaska before his time was up.

I learned some things about me on this trip. It was a great joy to walk alone among the gardens or the castle ruins. It was fun to take time to sit by myself in a seaside café and enjoy a latte and cookie while getting acquainted with the local restaurant manager. It was moving and nostalgic to sit on the wall facing the

Atlanta Ocean watching the waves come in and missing my Ned. And, it was great to laugh with others, meet new people, and share stories of families, fun, kids, and past adventures.

I also learned that I have become a really good listener. Most people who know me would tell you that I am always talking and that the center of attention is where I like to be – and they would be right about that.

However, in the years since Ned's death I have discovered listening as a profound gift to others and a unique and wonderful contribution to my life. On this trip it was much more important to me to hear than to be heard and as a result, I came home with some magical experiences.

More than once I was welcomed home in Ireland just because I was listening and was asked if I had Irish ancestors. When I shared that my great grandfather immigrated during the Potato Famine and that my new 23andMe test showed that I am 57.1% Irish, the response was "Welcome home!" It still moves me to tears to think about the connections I made in simple conversations sharing a table in a coffee shop or sitting next to someone on the bus or train or just talking with someone standing beside you sharing a breathtaking view of the Cliffs of Moher.

I missed Ned on the trip, but it was not a problem to be traveling alone. I loved the experience of discovering a new world and being in that world on my own. Travel alone. It is a new adventure you deserve. I am already planning my next journey. Alaska here I come…….

Signpost:

For the Widow:

Take time to listen and experience new adventures. There is much to learn and experience in the other's sharing and you have been given time to enjoy it. Don't waste the opportunity.

FINDING WHAT'S MISSING

In the first weeks and months after my husband's death, it seemed like nothing was the same and nothing would ever be the same again.

As it turns out, that really is true. Not everything is bad and nothing is the same.

Even my work is different without him to share the victories and the challenges. However, since about the middle of the second year I was aware that there was a hole in my life that I could not fill.

It was difficult to put my finger on what was missing because there was nothing wrong and yet there was just something that was not right. Obviously Ned was gone, and life was different. Many, many things had changed already, and I had managed to get through all the "firsts" that were part of the first year as a widow.

This was something different from just missing him. Of course, I missed him every day – and I still do – but there was just something else that I could not identify that was a kind of damper on life every day. It wasn't sad. It wasn't melancholy. It wasn't grief. In fact, for a long time all I had was a list of what it "wasn't" and no idea what it was.

After a couple of years, I thought maybe the thing that was missing was being around a man my age. I am the oldest of six children and the other five are brothers, so my mom and I lived in a house full of men. In addition, I have worked with men all my life and for 45 years shared every day with a man my age. Maybe I was just missing that relationship with men.

To test my theory, I did two different things. First, as I said earlier, I put a profile on a dating site for people over 55 and set up a few "coffee dates" to meet and greet men my age to talk and get acquainted. Of the six men I had coffee with, only one was of real interest and we had two or three dates at different coffee houses to talk and just appreciate the company. However, he was raising an 11-year-old granddaughter as his own child and I was not really interested in traveling that road again so "friends" is what we were and what we remain.

The others were definitely not the right person. One only wanted to talk about himself and the thing he was most proud of was that he bought a new car and after a year it only had 500 miles on it. I put 45,000 miles on my car in the last 18 months going and doing things with family and friends. Then, when there was a break in the monologue about himself and I started to share sometime about my life, he suddenly had to leave. Another one told me right up front he was interested in finding a "friend with benefits." When I told him I was up for the "friend" part but not the benefits, he thanked me, drank his coffee and left.

The one who was most interesting was the man who seemed to be very interested in me and my life until I answered his question about my career. I am an internationally-recognized expert in child sexual abuse prevention and a former practicing attorney. I teach adults how to recognize potential sexual predators in the environment and how to intervene and interrupt their grooming process, so children are safe. When I said that, he turned sideways in his chair and never made eye contact with me again. He started to squirm and suddenly had another appointment. I made him nervous and, I can honestly say he made me nervous too. In fact, I was on alert from the moment he sat down. Every instinct I had said this man was a risk. He left before I could find out more.

Even the one real date I had with a very nice guy was the most uncomfortable situation I had experienced in years. The whole time I was wishing I had my own car and could go home. After our date I sent him an email thanking him for the day and telling him that this was not the pathway for me.

This experiment taught me that dating was not going to lead me to what was missing so I tried something else. Perhaps, if the "missing" was having interesting men to talk to, I could find that somewhere else.

So, I went to a meeting of a local civic club meeting. It was fun and I got to spend an hour at the table with five older men who were interesting and fun to talk to and comfortable. It was a nice day and speaking with them was interesting and informative – and it did nothing to fill the "something's missing" hole.

For several years I wondered what it was that I could not see or find. I increased my workload, engaged in more community projects, took more time with grandchildren, and looked for new projects. Nothing seemed to fill the gap and the gap did not go away on its own. Then something unusual led me to what turned out to be "the" answer for me.

For almost 20 years while our children were growing up, we lived in Enid, Oklahoma – a farming community of about 40,000 people in northwest Oklahoma. We left that area for economic reasons during the oil bust in 1989 even though our friends and the life we built with our children were there. Ned's work opportunity was in Tulsa, so we packed up and moved. The two oldest kids were out of high school and Shannon was finishing her junior year when we left for Tulsa.

In the summer of 2017 I found out that my college roommate, who had also lived in Enid for a few years before we left and moved to Tulsa, was moving back to Enid.

I was surprised and curious as to why she made the decision to move back to Enid. She had lived elsewhere for 25 years - a lot longer than she had lived in Enid. When she got settled, she sent me a message that her guest room was ready, and she was looking forward to me coming over to just catch up for a couple of days.

We decided on a time, and on a Sunday afternoon in August, I headed west to see Carole and visit Enid again. In the years since Ned and I had moved away, I had made a few trips back. Erica lived in Enid for a few years as an adult and my best friend, Dorothy, was a significant part of my life until her death in 1993. Weddings, funerals, and special events kept me connected to Enid for several years but after a while my attention turned to things closer to Tulsa.

Now, I was making that two-hour trip on the Cimarron Turnpike once again.

As I drove into town and crossed the railroad tracks, I had a random thought. I heard myself asking "Now why was it we left here?" Of course, I knew why we moved, and it was necessary at the time but something else was starting to get provoked in that question.

As I drove into town, intending to meet Carole at the church we all attended, I found myself driving instead to the house Ned and I had lived in while we were in Enid. Suddenly, without thinking, I was sitting in my car in front of our Enid home. There was something peaceful and comforting about being back in the old neighborhood.

It felt like coming home.

I drove to the church where there was a potluck supper under way and when I walked in, I realized that of the 35 or so people in the room, I knew more than half of them. These were the people that were an integral part of our lives when Ned and I lived here and there was still a powerful connection. People were excited to see me and asked if I was moving back too.

Later that night as Carole and I were talking, I shared with her my experience of driving into town and how I felt when I got to the church that afternoon. The next day she asked me if I would consider moving back to Enid.

I can honestly say that had never crossed my mind. After all, by that time I had lived in Tulsa for 28 years – longer than we lived in Enid. So, I was stunned to hear myself say that I did not know.

There was something about the question that caused me to pause and look seriously at the possibility. The two and a half days I was in Enid were unsettling in some ways and comforting in others. As I drove around town, I had the experience of being at home and yet most of my family and my life was in Tulsa. Every person I saw that I knew from our time in Enid was thrilled to see me and excited at the prospect of me moving back. It seemed incredibly welcoming and oddly unsettling.

Turns out that a seed was planted that weekend that would lead me to discover what had been missing since Ned's death.

I headed home with a new question. Would I pull up stakes and move back to the place we raised our family?

It was not an easy question to answer. This was a major departure for me and there was a lot to consider. Shannon and her family moved to Tulsa because I was there. What would it mean for them if I moved to Enid?

Six of my grandchildren lived in Tulsa. How would a move to Enid impact my participation in their lives? There were boards and projects I was very involved with in Tulsa. Could I just turn that over to others and walk away from all that I built in that community?

For the next few weeks I considered these questions and prayed about it. I talked to friends about what I had been feeling since Ned's death and how being back in our old community had affected me.

After several days of thought, a good deal of prayer, and careful consideration, I realized that what was missing since Ned's death was a real sense of being "home." As long as Ned was alive, "home" was wherever he was. Once he died, that sense of being at home was missing for me.

When I looked then I realized that Tulsa was not "home" for me. I had really great relationships and wonderful experiences but for me Tulsa was a great place to visit. It was not "home." There were a few good friends in Tulsa but that did not make it home for me.

The kind of relationships that felt like "home" turned out to be waiting for me in a town two hours west of where I was living. So, in taking this trip to our former home I finally found what was missing since Ned's death and I decided to move HOME to Enid.

Before telling anyone else about my decision, I wrote a long email to my children and really shared with them all the spaces I had gone through in this process. They

knew I had been unsettled since Ned died. I talked with them about the fact that something was missing, and I had not yet discovered what it was. They encouraged me to keep looking, to try new things, and to look for ways to move forward. I don't think they expected my visit to Carole to trigger this kind of change – but it did.

The email shared the whole story of what I discovered was missing in my life and why I thought moving back to Enid was the right answer for me. The response I was most concerned about was that from my son, Ted.

Ted has never been big on change. He really likes things to stay the way they are. He has a great job and is a wonderful provider for his family and has only worked for about three companies in his entire life. He and Treasure and the kids still live in the "starter house" they bought after Kathlena was born and I know for a fact that he really did not accept that his Dad was gone until the day I actually turned our house over to the new owners.

However, I saw Ted the afternoon I came back from the trip to Enid and the visit with Carole and he remembered that all I could talk about was how being in Enid felt like home. A few minutes after I sent the email, I got a response from him saying he was not surprised at my decision. He heard it in my voice that day in August. He could tell that something that had been missing for me since Ned's death was now found and he wondered how long it would be before I was tell everyone what I had discovered and what I was going to do about it.

Erica and Shannon had similar responses. They wanted life and aliveness for me and really saw the move back to Enid as an opportunity for that. It was heartening to know that they all could see this was a good thing for me – and that what was good for my mental and physical health was good for the whole family.

The responses from my friends and family were varied. Some of my friends in Tulsa tried to talk me out of moving. One in particular was convinced this was an unwise decision and that I would regret it quickly. She thought I was moving away from my family. What she did not realize was that the person I was in Tulsa was not growing and not really living. I was going through the motions and I am grateful that my children could see that and understand my decision.

Another friend wanted to know if I met a man and was moving to be close to him. I think she was disappointed when I said "No!" Most of my friends were a bit confused but willing to listen and to make the effort to understand what I needed.

I took my time moving. There were things to complete in Tulsa and things to hand on to others before I could go. I was in the middle of dealing proactively with a special project that was going to take about six or seven months to resolve and I assured everyone that I would not move until that was complete.

There were issues to handle, projects to complete, responsibilities to hand on to the next person and decisions to be made about a number of matters. However, from the moment I announced I was moving to Enid everything changed. A new peace and tranquility filled my life and the smile on my face was infectious. Even those in Tulsa who were sad to see me go could not stay sad or mad about it because it was so clearly the right decision for me. No matter how much there was to do; no matter what challenges there were to getting moved; those around me could see that

I was truly happy for the first time since that day in March of 2011.

Things started to happen that let me know that moving back to Enid was the right thing to do from the very beginning.

For example, I looked at several options for places to live and finally decided on the condo complex where my college roommate was residing. I put my name on a waiting list knowing that it might be a while. After all, Carole had to wait a year to get into the complex. The plan was to find a different place that would work until the condo became available. However, about two months later, the owner of the complex called me and told me that the unit next door to my friend was open and that she knew that Carole and were friends and was offering it to me if I wanted it. I said "yes" and called Carole immediately. She told me that another couple was moving in on the other side of my unit that weekend. It was David and Cathe, friends for over 40 years.

I would be surrounded by friends in my new home. After I moved in, another friend of more than 40 years moved into the same complex right next door to my nearest neighbor.

My special project was to be finished on April 4th and I was planning to move on the 17th. The landlord let me know that my unit would be available on March 23rd (notice the date!). As a result, I was able to move all my major furniture and set up the new unit while I was working on finishing the project in Tulsa. Shannon,

Brianna, and Lachlann came with me to unpack one day during Spring Break and before I even moved the cabinets were full, the bed was made and ready, the china cabinet was unpacked, and the shower curtain was up. The new home was ready for me to settle in.

It might seem odd that the condo being ready three weeks before I was moving was good news but as I said, once I made the decision, things began to fall into place in many ways.

Shannon and Brian and I had started a corporate housing business and we were keeping the Tulsa duplex to rent out so moving my furniture the end of March meant that now I had two weeks to get the Tulsa place ready to rent furnished. We had the time to make sure the entire place was set up and ready to rent the day after I left – and it was occupied within a few days of my departure. On the 17th I brought the last load of my things over and settled in.

A few days later I was standing in my new the living room and suddenly realized that Ned helped the owner design these units many years ago. So here I was for the first time in my 45 years of being married to an architect living in something he designed – and surrounded by people I have known and cared about for more than 40 years. It felt like a dream come true.

The first Sunday I was at church people kept coming up to me welcoming me home and telling me how glad they were that I was there. I was being invited to participate in faith sharing groups, women's bible study, the music program, and a local P.E.O. chapter that was started by one of my oldest and dearest friends.

Everything in my life that seemed unsettled and disjointed before was now connected and "right." My finances were better. My health was great and keeps improving. My social life is ever expanding. There is joy and peace and love and care present everywhere. I am singing and creating new projects to make a difference and meeting new people.

Finding "home" again in Enid was nothing short of a miracle. I could not have made a better decision for me and the living of the rest of my life than moving back here. If I had listened to the naysayers in my life or even dismissed the idea of moving because I had been in Tulsa for 30 years, I would still be unsettled and struggling to create a new life.

Listening to my heart and trusting my instincts I am living a wonderful life with new and old friends. My daughter, Erica, reminded me that when you go where the Holy Spirit is directing you, things fall into place. It took me a few years to pay attention and I am grateful that I took the time to listen to what was best for me and the rest of my life.

That trip to see a long-time friend and take a couple of days to really reconnect was the best decision I'd made since March 23, 2011. I will be forever grateful for the invitation to come visit and for the Holy Spirit urging me to take a chance on this new adventure. Recognizing that something was missing and continuing to search until I found it has made all the difference in my life today.

If something seems to be missing for you, trust your instincts. Listen to that inner voice and look for your answer. Mine was to find a new "home." Yours could be anything. Look until you find it and trust yourself when you do. There are people in my life who were skeptical about this decision, but most of the people close to me saw that this is the right choice for me and that the only one who had to be sure about that was me.

Signpost:

For the Widow and For Others Experiencing Loss:

If you are experiencing something's missing in your life, look until you find it and then put it in. Living your life is what matters most after a profound loss. Only you can know what that will take.

MY NEW/OLD LIFE

There are many new things I am seeing about this altered life of mine – life as a "widowoman." For one thing, I am discovering that there are some similarities and some real differences between women who are single by choice and women who lived as part of a married couple and are now single because their spouse died.

All of them are single, so there are definitely some things that are the same. In my new/old life, there are women all around who fit both descriptions and they are teaching me some new things about connecting with others as a single woman when that's what I need and want.

Connecting with others is not a problem for me. I make friends easily and love being with people. However, I have noticed that I am not great at inserting myself in situations that are dominated by couples particularly if I am there alone. I often keep myself separate unless there is someone else I know there who is single. My friends who have lived single for many years are very adept and being comfortable in a world of "couples" and in making their way in the world as a single person.

My friend Dolores shared with me years ago that when her husband died, so did their social life with their couple friends. She was no longer part of a couple and the other "couples" did not seem to know how to include her without him. When you put that together with her dilemma of not knowing how to reinvent those couple relationships without him, her world got smaller – and so did mine. She had no trouble showing up at events or fundraisers or meetings but casual social gatherings went by the wayside. That was my experience after Ned died.

From my single "by choice" female friends I am learning something about what it takes to reinvent that social part of my life in a way that has me able to connect with couple friends from time to time without being uncomfortable or leaving anyone else in that space. It starts with me being willing to insert myself into situations that I would normally avoid –or at least wait to be invited to join. Even when I was married, I waited to be invited to join a group or an occasion. Speaking up and creating my own invitation is new territory and somewhat awkward for me.

I guess it is a little like teaching an old dog new tricks to expect someone over 70 to learn new rules of social interaction, but it is worth the effort. The couples and other single people I am reconnecting with are bringing new joy and fun to my life and reenergizing areas of life that have been long left untended and I am learning to ask for what I want and to not only invite myself to participate, but to invite others to join me.

Sometimes I have friends over for dinner. At times I invite couples I know and sometimes my single friends are the guests and sometimes both. I look forward to time with them and to being the lynchpin that brings people I know who don't know each other together to create new friendships and, in some cases, to renew old acquaintances.

Now it is me that's creating the space that brings people together. My single-by-choice friends are teaching me how to do that by their example. I can't thank them enough for taking me by the hand as I navigate new paths on this road.

A wonderful byproduct of this new aspect of the journey is that I have discovered since I moved here is that when my life is full and rich with interesting people and interesting things, the time I spend alone is also richer and more fulfilling. It's a win/win situation and I am grateful to all the new "teachers" I am encountering.

Signpost:

For the Widow and For Others Experiencing Loss:

Be open to new "teachers" in life. Sometimes when life takes a dramatic turn and you are faced with a new experience, people will show up to shine a light on the new pathway.

THE POWER OF SHARING

For over six years I have journeyed through this world of Widowhood. It is, as I have shared, a unique cultural phenomenon in our society. There are different aspects of this world that are experienced by almost all widows and some elements that are only present to some. However, for all of us, this world is a different space than the one we occupied before our husband died.

In the beginning I kept this new experience to myself. From time to time I shared with a close friend or with my children but for the most part I just wandered through this new territory looking for a path that worked for me. I could not see how sharing would help.

For several years my kids have encouraged me to write about this journey and share it with others. It is not that I was opposed to sharing. It is just that I did not think that sharing would make a difference. This was my journey. What could that mean to anyone else? Why was sharing this a good idea?

We human beings have a hard time with sharing. When we are children the idea of sharing means giving up something. When our parents or teachers tell us to "share" what they mean is give something of ours or something we have to someone else. That kind of "sharing" leaves me with less than what I had before - fewer toys, less candy, less time with another. Sharing does not occur for us as a way to lessen the grief or burden or a way to expand something. It just means I get less and have to give some of what I have to someone else.

As we grow up, sharing as a loss or risk is reinforced. We are asked to share our ideas with others – and then they take what we offer and present it as their own and again we lose. We share responsibilities – and then get left with the bulk of the job – and we are asked to share the burden with others who are suffering and in pain. As when we were children, sharing is not enlivening. It is not inspiring. It does not breathe life into us or life.

Then an opportunity shows up that can change our view. We are invited to share our experience of something for no reason other than to let others know that they are not alone and that there is something possible that did not seem possible before.

It is this new view of sharing that opened my eyes to what my children and friends were encouraging me to do – share my journey into widowhood. I started out writing a blog and ended up with this book.

As I finish the book, I realize the difference sharing with others has made for me. Sharing my widowhood journey has reminded me of the power of sharing. Every time I share about something that is part of my journey the impact on me is profound and the opportunity for others to make their own way is expanded. For example, sharing about widowhood and the holidays created a new opening for me to have a wonderful holiday season with none of the melancholy that has plagued the holidays for me since Ned's death. Sharing made something new possible and expanded the experience. In addition, the actions I am taking now to reinvent my life are easy and graceful for me and for most of those around me because I have been authentically sharing with everyone what I am up to and why I am doing it.

In this effort, sharing has decreased the pain and grief of life in this new world and has allowed me to open my heart to others. Even when some have said that they disagree with something I said it becomes clear that the sharing is what matters. I have said many times that this is not how it "is" to be a widow. This is what *my* journey is like and I hope that sharing it with others has opened the door for them to share their journey with the people in their lives.

Sharing in this context has power and promotes health and well-being. It offers the chance for others to examine their own experience and look for themselves at how life is going for them as they travel this new road.

Sharing for me has opened the door to a new experience. It has provided an outlet for expressing all the roadblocks I have encountered and the hurdles that seem to crop up on society's roadway. Simply saying what's there for me and continuing to remind everyone that it is my experience – not necessarily everyone's – has also opened the door for others to be in communication.

In this context, sharing begets sharing and new life comes from letting go of the experiences that keep us trapped and from sharing the new worlds we are creating and discovering. Take the chance and share.

Someone will listen and a new world can open up for both of you.

Signpost:

For the Widow and For Others Experiencing Loss:

Don't be afraid to share your experience. It will make a difference for you and for others.

IT'S UNIMAGINABLE

You know, one of the most authentic things said to me since Ned's death is "I can't imagine what it must be like."

It's true. Unless you have been down this path, you can't imagine. I know because I tried to imagine what it would be like.

Ned was next in a long line of Doty men who had died at age 56 so he lived life as if that would be the end for him too. He always told me that he would not be around long and encouraged me to create a life that could go on after he was gone. After all, he had already been diagnosed with the same health issues that resulted in their deaths at age 56. So, from time to time when he was gone on a trip out of town for a few days, I tried to imagine what it would be like to live life without him. No matter what I thought it would be like, this is not that.

Of course, there are things I could imagine like actually being alone. But most things I have experienced and dealt with were unimaginable. Even the things I thought I knew would be there did not show up the way I expected.

For example, here I am several years later still discovering things that he handled with grace and ease that I am bumbling through. Those moments often find me talking to him and letting him know how annoying it is that he left when he did. But that's different than being on this journey into widowhood.

Don't get me wrong, I can do what I need to do. I am perfectly capable of dealing with whatever comes along – as I know most women are. We are nothing if not resilient and if I have learned anything since his death it is that the road is different for each of us.

My path is not the same as the next woman's and hers is different from the next one. Each of us is on our own journey into Widowhood. Writing about it has made a huge difference in my freedom to be with all that life now holds for me. It has opened the door to me seeing things I have not seen before and to creating a new life for the rest of my years. But, it is my journey.

A friend of mine whose husband was one of Ned's closest friends lost her husband a few years after Ned died. He too had a stroke that had a devastating impact on him. She read some things I wrote about my experience in a blog I was writing at the time and called me one day to say that she did not really know how to respond. When I just said "Okay", she was a bit confused. Then I told her that whether it is the book or the blog, what I was sharing was my experience. And, I was sharing it in the hope that she (and you) would have the freedom to share your journey with others too.

If my journey speaks to you or to her or to anyone, that's great. If it gives you permission to acknowledge your own experience and take actions that serve and support you, that's great. If my words are affirming for you, that's great and if what I have to offer is nothing like what you are dealing with, that's great too.

This book is my journey. I share it so that others can be affirmed by my experience and see that some of the things that they have encountered as a widow are just a part of our culture that is truly hidden from view.

I also share it so that the rest of society can begin to understand how their words and actions toward women dealing with the loss of a spouse sometimes have a different impact than intended. It seems as if that scriptural reference "Pity the poor widow" has become part of the background of life for society. My intention is to shine a light on that culture so that society can see how it sometimes diminishes "widowomen" and treats us as if we are not capable.

As I write these words, I am present to a life I could not have imagined. As I embark on each new adventure, I am particularly grateful for all the years of loving and sharing I had with Ned. We walked a faith filled, loving, and interesting road and though there were rough spots on the trip, I am grateful for every step we took together and I promise that the rest of my journey will honor the faith he had in me that I could and would live an unimaginable life for the rest of my time on this planet.

To Ned:

Thanks, my love, for loving me forever and always and for constantly reminding me that I am enough and that there are no limits to what I can accomplish. Since the day we met you have been and you are still the wind beneath my wings!

Made in the USA
Coppell, TX
15 July 2020

31052923R00103